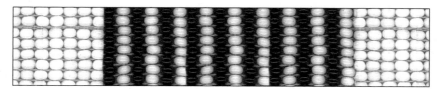

FROM THE **Iron House**

Aboriginal Studies Series

Aboriginal Studies is still a neglected area in Canada; we need to know more about events like Oka and other Aboriginal resistance movements, and about Aboriginal people and their relationships with others. This series is designed to create a meeting ground of knowledge for Aboriginals and non-Aboriginals alike, and to highlight Aboriginal voices so that we may learn more about one another and speak with one another with a richer understanding.

We are seeking manuscripts that are interdisciplinary or cross-disciplinary in approach, with an emphasis on oral traditions and oral narratives, literature, history, law, film, and politics.

Please send inquiries to the Series co-editors:

Dr. Ute Lischke
Department of Languages
    and Literature
Wilfrid Laurier University
75 University Avenue West
Waterloo, ON N2L 3C5
Phone: (519) 884–0710 ext. 3607
Fax: (519) 884–7369
Email: ulischke@wlu.ca

Dr. David T. McNab
School of Arts and Letters
Atkinson Faculty of Liberal
    and Professional Studies
York University
608 Atkinson College
4700 Keele Street
Toronto, ON M3J 1P3
Phone: (416) 736–2100 ext. 22423
Fax: (416) 736–5766
Email: dtmcnab@yorku.ca

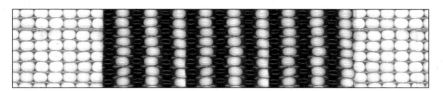

FROM THE Iron House

Imprisonment in First Nations Writing

Deena Rymhs

ABORIGINAL STUDIES SERIES

Wilfrid Laurier University Press
[WLU]

This book has been published with the help of a grant from the Canadian Federation for the Humanities and Social Sciences, through the Aid to Scholarly Publications Programme, using funds provided by the Social Sciences and Humanities Research Council of Canada. We acknowledge the financial support of the Government of Canada through the Book Publishing Industry Development Program for our publishing activities.

Library and Archives Canada Cataloguing in Publication

Rymhs, Deena, 1975–
    From the iron house : imprisonment in First Nations writing / Deena Rymhs.

(Aboriginal studies series)
Includes bibliographical references and index.
ISBN 978-1-55458-021-7

    1. Prisoners' writings, Canadian (English)—History and criticism. 2. Canadian literature (English)—Indian authors—History and criticism. 3. Imprisonment in literature. 4. Indians of North America—Canada—Residential schools. 5. Indians in literature. 6. Canadian literature (English)—20th century—History and criticism. I. Title. II. Series: Aboriginal studies series (Waterloo, Ont.)

PS8089.5.I5R95 2008   C810.9'355308997   C2007-906849-9

Cover design by David Drummond. Text design by Catharine Bonas-Taylor.

This book is printed on Ancient Forest Friendly paper (100% post-consumer recycled).

Printed in Canada

Published by Wilfrid Laurier University Press
Waterloo, Ontario, Canada
www.wlupress.wlu.ca

for Betty Rymhs

Contents

Acknowledgements

This book is, in part, the culmination of the energy and dedication of individuals other than myself. My sincere thanks go to Glenn Willmott for nurturing this project in its various stages. Laura Murray's sharpness brought an intellectual deftness to this study. The two anonymous readers reviewing the manuscript contributed to the breadth and readability of this book; I am grateful to have had their critical engagement at the prepublication stage. Lisa Quinn and, indeed, all the people at Wilfrid Laurier University Press have been superlative at what they do. I cannot imagine a more positive relationship between author and press. I also wish to thank the Department of English at St. Francis Xavier University for taking a gamble on me that played no small part in the completion of this book.

Sections of this book originally appeared in *English Studies in Canada, Auto/biography in Canada: Critical Directions* (ed. Julie Rak), *Genre: Forms of Discourse and Culture, Canadian Literature,* and *Essays on Canadian Writing,* and are reprinted here with permission.

My family and friends deserve my whole gratitude for their constant commitment and affection. Roger, Betty, and Trisha offered endless support. Sandra Neill and Robert Luke have been inspirations. Yaël Schlick's generosity in my latter years of graduate work is something for which I have always been grateful. Finally, I would be remiss to leave out Christopher, whose gentle encouragement and confidence in me will take me from this book and beyond.

Introduction

What Is Carceral Writing?

In a "small, juvenile female cage" with "green cement floor, faded yellow cement walls and ceiling," Yvonne Johnson surveys her prison cell from a thin plastic mattress (Wiebe and Johnson 368). She is awaiting a jury's verdict in a North Battleford prison after providing testimony against her brother for rape. As she observes her surroundings, she notes the names of its past occupants inscribed around her. The markings rise out from their illicit spaces and begin to speak a history: "Their names are everywhere, scratched, cut deep into the bunks, the yellow walls. Relatives I recognize from storytelling, or a chance meeting, family friends whom I may have met once on Red Pheasant. If I worked at it, my name here would be recognized as a Johnson of the John Bear family" (368). As she pieces together a history from these scrawlings, she laments, "Sad ... to search prison walls for news of one's own people; to become like an archaeologist trying to read the stones of tombs about the lives of your own ancient dead" (368). The names left behind are a record, a proxy history of intersecting lives and lost kinships. That Johnson, who spent most of her life in Butte, Montana, recognizes the names scratched into a North Battleford prison wall underscores the prevalent role that penal and regulatory institutions have played in the recent histories of Aboriginal people. Gesturing toward a powerful oral history, Johnson's recognition also indicates a collective awareness and memory that exist independently of the written form. As would seem fitting, the prison walls have become a medium for this history, a narrative that emerges from the undersides of bunks. The markings signify a counter-discourse, a quiet and intractable conversation carried out among this structure's occupants.

As this passage from Yvonne Johnson and Rudy Wiebe's *Stolen Life: The Journey of a Cree Woman* suggests, the prison is not just an apparatus of detention and punishment, but a structure signifying the colonization, criminalization, and suppression of a people. The personal histories of indigenous people in Canada are so heavily entangled in carceral institutions that it is difficult to discuss the former without the latter. This relationship is starkly reflected in the staggering numbers of Aboriginal inmates. In Canada, Aboriginal people constitute the largest incarcerated minority in federal, provincial, and territorial correctional facilities. While they make up roughly 3 percent of the general population, they account for 18 percent of the federal prison population (Canada, Office of the Correctional Investigator 11). This disproportion is far greater in the Prairie provinces and Ontario, where Aboriginal prison populations are seven to ten times greater than the provincial average (Statistics Canada 16). The prologue to this overrepresentation is the political and economic disempowerment of Aboriginal groups. The disproportionate rate of incarceration is thus emblematic of the historically fraught relationship between First Nations people and the state.

With its parallel, insidious presence in the recent histories of Aboriginal people, the residential school has also been likened to a prison. These institutions played a regulatory and punitive function that instilled a similar sense of cultural guilt. While their intrusion into the lives of their occupants was not the result of individual violations of the Criminal Code, their operations resembled those of prisons. Children entering residential schools were typically stripped of their personal effects, clothed in uniforms, and renamed or assigned numbers. These practices instilled institutional order and docility in the occupants and at the same time effaced their prior identity. Both the residential school and the prison used surveillance as a means of control. In his memoir *Indian School Days*, Anishnabe author Basil Johnston describes being under constant watch:

> The eyes began their surveillance in the morning, watching the washing of hands and faces. The eyes followed all movements in the dressing of the beds; the eyes were transfixed on the backs of worshippers during mass. Throughout the day the eyes traced the motions of hands at table; the eyes glared at the figures bent and coiled in work; the eyes

tracked [...] the movement of feet during play; [...] the eyes censored letters received and letters written. The eyes, like those of the wolf, peered in the dark in watch over still, sleeping forms. The eyes were never at rest. (138)

Even the most private activities, such as bathing and sleeping, Johnston reveals, were subject to observation. This method of control was invasive, penetrative even. In her residential school autobiography, Cree author Jane Willis recalls being forced to consume a laxative on her arrival at the residential school to purge her insides. "Our insides too had to be sterilized, just like our bodies," she remarks, revealing that even their innermost functions were subject to regulation (44). While such descriptions may call to mind more universal experiences of public school education—for instance, one might compare these scenes to those found in George Orwell's account of his British schooling—the cultural values on which residential schools were founded set these institutions apart from the British public school or North American private school. These episodes have a much different resonance for their authors. Operating within an aggressive colonizing agenda, the residential school produced an experience so distinct that, years later, subsequent generations would be working through the cultural damage these institutions left in their wake. The guilt experienced by residential school occupants invites comparison with the type of criminalization described by the prison authors of this study. Basil Johnston implies this likeness when he remarks, "Our treatment implied that we were little better than felons or potential felons" (138).

In addition to operating in a similar way, the residential school has been seen as prefiguring the prison. "Placed in a historical context," the Committee of the Canadian Bar Association concluded in 1988, "the prison has become for many young native people the contemporary equivalent of what the Indian residential school represented for their parents" (in York 146–47). Some critics place the residential school and the prison on a continuum with one another in their containment of Aboriginal youth and in the similar type of cultural rupture they produced. In her autobiographical collaboration with established Canadian author Rudy Wiebe, written while she was serving a twenty-five-year sentence for murder, Yvonne Johnson remarks, "I was my mother thirty years later" (200) as she underlines the semblance between her mother's personal history and her own. Johnson likens her imprisonment to her mother's experience in the "the religious jail" or residential school (200). Similarly, Anishnabe-Lakota activist Leonard Peltier, serving two life sentences in Leavenworth Federal Penitentiary, Kansas, for the murder of two FBI officers, speaks of his entry into the Wahpeton boarding school as his "first imprisonment" (78).

The guilt engrained in the children, Peltier suggests, would come to characterize their later dealings with legal institutions. These examples posit the residential school as an antecedent to the prison, as the first place where guilt is experienced. Many of the authors in this study return to these continuities between the residential school and the prison, pointing to their joint function along a larger carceral continuum.

Other critics have turned their attention to the child welfare system in Canada and contend that the disproportionate removal of Aboriginal children from their families is a continuation of the residential school legacy. Kanien'keheka law professor Patricia Monture-Angus sees the child welfare system "as being on a continuum with the criminal justice system" (194). She explains: "The child welfare system feeds the youth and adult correctional systems. Both institutions remove citizens from their communities, which has a devastating effect on the cultural and spiritual growth of the individual. It also damages the traditional social structures of family and community" (194). Monture-Angus argues that the child welfare system creates future offenders while eroding the social and cultural fabric of indigenous communities. Her arguments inform this book's later reading of Métis author James Tyman's autobiography, *Inside Out*, in which Tyman explores his adoption into a White, middle-class family and the effect of the racism he experienced within his adoptive environment on his subsequent criminal activities. Tyman's autobiography insists that Aboriginal child custody issues be recognized as intertwined with the carceral histories of indigenous people.

A number of Aboriginal critics and political writers further this notion of incarceration as a cultural condition. Harry Daniels, past president of the Native Council of Canada (now the Congress of Aboriginal Peoples), remarks on the prison's insidious presence in the post-contact histories of indigenous people. "One day the whole of the Native population will at some point in their lives be incarcerated," he estimates, "whether it be in foster homes, residential schools, reform schools, provincial, federal, or territorial prisons" (Native Council of Canada vi–vii). Daniels extends this state of confinement to the 1977 socio-economic state of Aboriginal people. He sees the overrepresentation of Aboriginal people in prison as an explicit reminder of the limited social and economic mobility of indigenous people outside prison. The proximity between Aboriginal people inside and outside the prison is underscored by Monture-Angus when she remarks, "I have often been amazed that I landed at law school in Kingston, Ontario, only eight blocks (or so) from the federal Prison for Women. I have always felt that I should have properly landed on the other side of that high limestone wall" (47–48). Monture-Angus sees this carceral continuum as an acting force on Aboriginal people, a type of historical patterning that virtually predetermines their lives. A female prisoner interviewed in Fran Sugar and Lana Fox's *Survey of Federally Sentenced Aboriginal Women in the Community* develops Monture-Angus's sentiments further when she points out the fraught relationship between Aboriginal people and agents of authority: "As children we were taught to fear white authority because of the punishments it could enforce. Faced with institutional neglect and overt racism, our feelings about white authority even before we encountered the criminal justice system mixed passive distrust with active hatred" (11). Such tensions precede the actual experience of incarceration and structure Aboriginal peoples' subsequent encounters with legal institutions. These statements reinforce the view of imprisonment as a collectively known experience.

Just as schools and adoptive families have been experienced as prisons, even home, the reserve, in its physical segregation, curtailing of indigenous territory, and concentration of economic poverty, has been compared to a prison. This relation is encapsulated in the title of Howard Adams's 1975 work, *Prison of Grass*, a study of the physical, ideological, and economic containment of Aboriginal peoples in Canada. Supposedly, reserves guaranteed a land base for indigenous communities; in fact, they limited those communities to often marginal lands for the benefit of White society's agricultural and industrial expansion. For some reserve communities, the isolation becomes a sort of prison, a place their youth wish to escape. In Tomson Highway's *Kiss of the Fur Queen*, a semi-autobiographical novel about the Cree playwright's residential schooling in Manitoba, and Jane Willis's *Geniesh*, a residential school autobiography set in northern Quebec and Ontario, the main characters leave their isolated communities for the residential school. However strong their fear of leaving the reserve, both characters are seduced by the idea of the world outside it. These are narrative instances of the phenomenon, identified by Geoffrey York and Rupert Ross in their studies of Aboriginal people and the law, of an increasing desire among Aboriginal youth to escape their remote and often hopeless contexts. Out of a sense of confinement and boredom, York and Ross point out, youth sometimes commit crimes in order to escape the reserve and to enter the outside world through the medium of a detention centre.

So pervasive is the experience of imprisonment in the recent histories of First Nations people that several authors make it a theme of their writing. In "Justice," Mi'kmaq poet Rita Joe offers a poetic reflection on the troubled relationship between Aboriginal people and the law. She describes the mien of this Western institution: "Justice seems to have many faces / It does not want to play if my skin is not the right hue" (1–2). Joe's personification of this value undermines its claims to impartiality. Instead, she emphasizes its injurious history: "Justice is like an open field / We observe, but are afraid to approach" (5–6). She continues: "Hence the broken stride / And the lingering doubt" (8–9). In this short meditation on Western justice, Joe explains the damaging role the institutions of justice have played in the lives of Aboriginal people. Showing how justice is implicated in a violent and colonial history, she criticizes this apparently universal value.

Rita Joe's poem "Lament of Donald Marshall Jr." presents an equally critical view of justice. Like Rita Joe, Donald Marshall is Nova Scotian Mi'kmaq. Convicted of murder at the age of seventeen, he served eleven years in prison before his acquittal in 1983. The Royal Commission examining his case attributed his wrongful conviction to police and prosecutorial misconduct, incompetent defence counsel, perjured testimony, jury bias, and a rushed trial.[1] Marshall has emerged as an important symbol for Aboriginal people of the criminal justice system's failure to prosecute fairly. His story resonates with that of Leonard Peltier, who also serves as a spectral figure for many of the writers in this study. Peltier, who was convicted of murdering two FBI officers on the Pine Ridge reservation in 1975, has become, for many, synonymous with the continued persecution of indigenous peoples and with the legal and judicial systems' denial of justice for them. Joe's song emphasizes Marshall's treatment in the context of this broader, collective condition: "My hurt it is known, it is known the world over," the song repeats (12). Ending each verse is the refrain, "We are the same, we are the same, we are the same, we are the same" (15). This repetition produces the impression that these pleas are unheard and that the justice system's failure of Aboriginal people will continue.

The justice system's negative impact on indigenous people is the subject of Art Solomon's "Wheels of Injustice," a poem that describes the wheels of justice grinding away "the hopes and / dreams" of Aboriginal people, who provide the fodder for penal machinery. Solomon, an Anishnabe Elder who has mentored Aboriginal prisoners in Canadian prisons, helped usher Aboriginal spiritual practices into prisons and secure the recognition of those practices as a fundamental right of prisoners. His poem carries out a trenchant critique of the legal-judicial system by questioning its ability to live up to the Christian principles of the dominant society. In *Prison Writings*, Leonard Peltier takes a similar tack, abandoning his exhausted pleas of innocence and turning attention to the denial of truth, justice, and mercy that he maintains characterized his trial. First Nations leaders and delegates employed a similar rhetorical strategy in their early correspondence with colonial dignitaries. In a 1786 letter to Lord Sydney, Kanien'kehaka chief Joseph Brant wrote: "The palaces and prisons among you form a most dreadful contrast. Go to the former places, and you will see perhaps a *deformed piece of earth* assuming airs that become none to the Great Spirit above. Go to one of your prisons; here description utterly fails! […] and how do you call yourselves Christians?" (in Petrone, *First People* 37). Like Solomon and Peltier, Brant questions the values that undergird European prison systems. Drawing attention to the conditions and practices of these penal structures, he calls into question their founding precepts. Many Aboriginal writers follow in this tradition to expose the fraudulent nature of the justice system, showing that it is not blind, is not merciful, and does not always protect the rights of those with whom it is entrusted.

As Brant's letter indicates, much First Nations literature proceeds from a tradition of protest writing that seeks to address, among other things, the historical criminalization of indigenous people and the use of institutions such as prisons to wear away at their cultural identity. In *Native Literature in Canada*, Penny Petrone argues: "The literature of Canada's native peoples has always been quintessentially political, addressing their persecutions and betrayals and summoning their resources for resistance. The political dimension is an inherent part of their writing because it is an inherent part of their lives" (182). This statement highlights Native writing's oppositional stance, from its early inception as appeals, letters, and petitions to royalty and government to more recent, personal literary forms such as autobiography and poetry. While not all Aboriginal literature in Canada is protest writing—for instance, many traditional oral genres and pre-contact expressive forms exceed this classification—the political element that Petrone emphasizes is fundamental to understanding a large part, though not all, of this literature's post-contact developments. Cree-Métis scholar Emma LaRocque echoes Petrone's characterization of indigenous writing. "Much of Native writing," she points out, "whether blunt or subtle, is protest literature in that it speaks to the process of our colonization: dispossession, objectification, marginalization, and that constant struggle for cultural survival expressed in the movement for structural and psychological self-determination" (xviii). As explicit instances of this protest tradition identified by Petrone and LaRocque, the prison texts examined in this book represent a core component of Aboriginal literature generally and writing of the past three decades specifically.

This book explores the impact of the prison and the residential school on the recent histories of Aboriginal people. Drawing from international theory on prison writing, literary criticism on Aboriginal writing, and adjacent theoretical discussions of testimony, memoir, and confession, my work attempts to build, from the ground up, a conceptual framework for examining this significant yet little studied body of writing. Two bodies of literature provide the focus of this book: writing by authors who are or have been incarcerated, and works written about the residential school.

Both point to the pervasive theme of imprisonment in Aboriginal literature. Curiously, however, literature dealing with the experience of imprisonment has yet to receive a book-length study of this kind. There exists
on an even more general scale a meager amount of scholarship on prison
writing in Canada. This critical oversight is identified by Ioan Davies, who
points out that while prison writing from other nations has received attention in this country, "its own prison writing does not become part of its own
literary or philosophical sense" (7). Davies's argument, to be sure, would
need to be adjusted to describe Aboriginal literature, which is conscious
of the prison's prominence in indigenous peoples' lives. From this latter
viewpoint, the prison experience is not "part of a criminal subculture," in
Davies's words, but "part of an entire dispossessed culture" (127). Yet in
terms of the reception of Aboriginal prison writing by readers of a dominant culture, why is prison literature, as Davies puts it, "at the margin of
our discourses?" (221). How do we make sense of the lack of attention to
literature dealing with the experience of imprisonment, given the consid-
erable volume of this writing and this literature's acute reflection of the troubled relationship between Aboriginal people and the law?

While this book is in many ways inaugural in its subject matter, it
draws on critical frameworks developed in political as well as literary contexts. The marginal place this writing occupies in the Canadian public
imagination might be considered next to the geopolitical space from which
Aboriginal writing emerges. The concept of the "Fourth World" gained
currency in 1975 during the First General Assembly of the World Council of Indigenous Peoples (WCIP) and was first introduced by George
Manuel, leader of the National Indian Brotherhood, and Michael Posluns
in their 1974 book *The Fourth World: An Indian Reality*. Advocating for
indigenous rights within a global community of nation-states, the Fourth
World collectively refers to "minority ethnic groups [who] are the subject
of internal colonialism" (Graburn 1). At once real, imagined, political, and
material, the Fourth World is a defining concept for indigenous peoples,
whose histories and present realities set them apart from the First World
nations they occupy. While the Fourth World has been contested by some
post-colonial critics for overlooking the vast, historically situated struggles
of colonized groups and for failing to recognize international hierarchies
within individual cultures,[2] Manuel's vision of the Fourth World offered
a profound alternative for indigenous people in Canada, one that illumi-
nated a geopolitical identity beyond the boundaries of the nation. A blue-
print for a new political consciousness, the Fourth World signified an
important "rejection of the models of social, technological, and economic
development implicit in the idea of the Third World, where the imagery
of underdevelopment is the underlying premise" (Hall 240). This con-

cept's enduring value is that it recognizes indigenous peoples' shared political situations and the potential for empowering collaboration. The narrative project of the Fourth World, Chadwick Allen further explains, is the
development of an "autoethnography that both engages and attempts to
counter the First World's dominant discourses of master narrative and ethnic taxonomy" (237). The collective identification imagined by the Fourth
World helps us place Aboriginal writing in Canada and in other global
contexts. It gives us a framework for approaching this literature that orig-
inates from a unique political space.

In post-colonial terms, Aboriginal writing also represents a "minority
discourse," the often occluded body of expression whose "figurations of
values [are] radically opposed to those of the dominant culture" (JanMohamed and Lloyd 8) and whose goal is to "negate the prior hegemonic
negation of itself" (10). Minority texts often flow out of injurious, even
genocidal, histories. "Given such a historically sustained negation of minority voices, we must first realize that minority discourse is, in the first
instance, the product of damage," JanMohamed and Lloyd propose (4).
These two critics see minority writing as responding to various types of
institutional suppression. While wary of facile groupings of different
minority cultures, post-colonial studies of minority discourse acknowledge
similar struggles for political autonomy and self-representation, "drawing out solidarities in the form of similarities between modes of repression
and struggle that all minorities experience separately but experience pre-
cisely as minorities" (9). Such affinities often involve an engagement with
dominant constructions that threaten to disempower or silence minority
cultures—for instance, the representation of minority cultures as "underdeveloped, imperfect, childlike" or "inauthentic, perverse, or criminal"
(4–5). The construction of the Other as deviant and of its literature as
underdeveloped is particularly relevant to the writing examined in this
book. The authors featured in this study explore the historical criminalization of Aboriginal people while implicitly addressing their slighting
by audiences of a dominant culture.

Post-colonial theory provides a lens for reading indigenous literature;
the carceral writings examined in this book also raise worthwhile questions
for post-colonial studies. Where post-colonial frameworks, particularly
those used in Canadian contexts, have been faulted for their limited reliance
on a colony–empire paradigm (Sugars 103), the literature discussed in the
following chapters points to locations of writing that exceed this binary.
This writing confronts current colonialisms, the continued oppression of
indigenous people within settings such as the prison that are granted state-
sanctioned authority to punish Aboriginal subjects. How do authors writing from such a place disentangle themselves from the public scorn

associated with it? Many of the authors examined in this book speak from an "overdetermined" position, a place that they insist is already infused with guilt. Leonard Peltier pleads his individual innocence in the crimes of which he was convicted, but he also insists that innocence does not exist for Aboriginal people within the American justice system. His guilt he attributes directly to institutional racism; his only crime, he puts it, is "being an Indian" (15). James Tyman, too, suggests this inherent state of guilt when he remarks sardonically, "'I was born criminal, I guess'" (129). This inherent state of guilt is the basis on which these authors critique the legal-judicial system. The feeling of being branded guilty mediates the authors' appeals to their readerships, influencing, in part, whom they envision that readership to be, and challenging the belief that they can ever vindicate themselves entirely. Similarly, the residential school authors in this book draw attention to the guilt engrained in them during their time in these institutions, a guilt correlated with race. Reframing our understanding of guilt and innocence, these authors write from what is in many ways a space of inalienable difference. Prison authors, moreover, have to contend with the moral condemnation levelled at them as publicly convicted writers.

In addition to its intersections with minority literature and Fourth World criticism, this book is also indebted to an existing body of criticism on resistance writing. Though devoted primarily to the writings of international political detainees, Barbara Harlow's work on resistance literature offers a critical model for recognizing how Aboriginal prison writing reflects a collective enterprise and struggle, how it intervenes in the historical record, and how it challenges traditional understandings of literature. Harlow makes the case that prison writing plays a unique role in producing a counter-discourse: "Penal institutions, despite, if not because of, their function as part of the state's coercive apparatus of physical detention and ideological containment, provide the critical space within which, indeed from out of which, alternative social and political practices of counter-hegemonic resistance movements are schooled" (*Barred* 10). Harlow emphasizes the contribution of prison writing to political movements outside the prison. Her recognition of the prison as a seedbed of political consciousness and social activism enriches one's reading of the literature in this study. Some of the prison authors in this book are actively involved with political movements outside the prison. Canadian criminologist Robert Gaucher underlines the role that indigenous prisoners have played in outside movements: "In Canada, aboriginal prisoners were involved with and informed by the American Indian Movement from its formative stages as illustrated in the organizing of prison Native Brotherhoods and Sisterhoods, their newsletters, magazines, and political pronouncements"

("Inside Looking Out" 40). Aboriginal prisoners may be peripheral to intellectual dialogues in this country; even so, their writing represents a significant if underestimated voice both domestically and globally.

This book also finds similar textual practices between the writings of imprisoned Aboriginal authors and the detained authors Ioan Davies writes about in *Writers in Prison*. Davies focuses largely on prison writers who are part of revolutionary movements, arguing that "in virtually all cases, prison or exile has provided the opportunity for the reformulation of ideas in such a way that they had profound implications for the direction of the political movement. The relationship of prison writing to revolutionary movement is thus a crucial one" (54). While Davies's interest is in intellectual prison authors who are part of revolutionary movements, my study deals largely with the "common criminal," or authors who become writers out of their imprisonment. Davies's focus on the archetypes and motifs that emanate from "the incarcerated imagination" also assumes a writing subject outside of history. A discussion of the prison's valence for Aboriginal communities is largely absent from Davies's study. The Aboriginal authors examined in this book question notions of guilt and innocence. Exploring the racialized dimensions of guilt, they insist that there is no recourse to proving their innocence in this system, within which their guilt seems preassigned. These writers frequently construct a continuum between themselves and Aboriginal populations outside the prison.

The continuum these authors construct calls to mind Michel Foucault's theory of "the carceral"—the multiple and often overlapping sites of discipline that define delinquency and that naturalize the power to punish. Foucault explains how disciplinary power is diffused throughout the social space. He treats the prison and the school, along with other settings such as the factory, the military, and the hospital, as homologous institutions that function within a network of social control. "The prison is merely the natural consequence," Foucault maintains, "no more than a higher degree, of that hierarchy laid down step by step" (301). The carceral continuum laid out in Foucault's *Discipline and Punish* is a real, acting force over many of the authors in this book. In many ways, Yvonne Johnson is in prison before she is in prison. Like many of the prison authors featured in the first half of this book, Johnson explores her lack of choices before her imprisonment. Noting the similarities between her mother's residential schooling and her own incarceration, Johnson goes on to suggest how imprisonment is a familiar state for Aboriginal people. Even though the experiences described by these authors correspond to Foucault's theory of the carceral, however, his discussion of discipline needs to be historically situated if we are to account for the various roles that the prison has played for different cultural communities. One might propose, in answer to this problem, that the mechanisms of discipline Foucault describes—observation, collation of records, institutional control—are more heightened for certain racial groups. Still, Foucault neglects to address in any explicit way how racial bodies are marked differently as they move through sites of disciplinary power. Although his theories recognize that power is corporeally based, they fail to address, as Gail Weiss points out, "the definite ways in which bodies are marked by assumptions made about their gender, their race, their ethnicity, [and] their class" (2). Foucault's argument about the individualizing effects of the prison further overlooks the collective identities that many of these authors articulate and construct in their works—identities that extend beyond the prison. While this book proceeds from Foucault's ideas of the carceral, then, the literature featured in this study makes an important contribution to—and tests the limits of—Foucault's framework.

There is another community on whose behalf the prisoner may speak, and that is a prisoner or convict community. Criticism of prison literature in the West has typically described this prison culture in universal terms. South African author and former political detainee Breyten Breytenbach writes: "When you are interested in prison accounts as a genre you will soon see that prisons are pretty much the same the world over. It is [...] the peculiar relationship of power-repression which seems immutable, wherever you may hide" (339). The uniformity of the prison environment, Breytenbach implies, produces a uniformity in the accounts produced from it. Prison author Michael Hogan also describes the prisoner's experience in universal terms: "One of the constants for any prisoner is the singularity with which he enters when incarcerated, an existence whose periphery is both violent and insane" (91). In this setting, Hogan argues, the prisoner's response is to seek out a sense of community. The pull toward unity, Hogan explains, is more a human than a political impulse, a reaction to the singularity and isolation this environment evokes. However, Hogan's and Breytenbach's emphasis on the universal experiential dimensions of the prison neglects to address the different directions the prisoner's identification may take. Hogan's insistence on a type of brotherhood separated from a cultural and political consciousness fails to acknowledge the influences, prior to and during incarceration, that determine how this brotherhood might be expressed. Specifically, it minimizes the tensions that exist among different racial groups in the prison. Salish-Kootenai scholar Luana Ross counters this uniform thinking of prison experience in *Inventing the Savage: The Social Construction of Native American Criminality*. "Cultural pluralism has not worked in Euro-American society," Ross points out, "and undoubtedly does not operate inside the prison. As a technique of control, racial/ethnic groups are encouraged to foster antagonistic relationships" (155). During his time in prison, James Tyman noted this antagonism between White and Aboriginal inmates, the latter of whom represented a prison majority. Observing the denigration of a young White prisoner by Aboriginal prisoners, Tyman remarked: "I'd been expecting raw behavior, but the racism was blatant" (103). While the desire for brotherhood may affect each inmate similarly, as Hogan argues, this brotherhood may take different forms.

Other critics address the relation between different prison cultures in a way that emphasizes their coexistence. In his study of American prison literature, H. Bruce Franklin sees a White and, in his assessment, predominantly individualistic convict tradition as having a continuing influence on the writing produced in prisons. American prison literature, he argues, reveals an underlying dialectic "between a collective revolutionary consciousness based on a Black historical experience and the loneliness of the isolated convict ego, branded or cast out, seeking either to reintegrate with the social order or to defy it in anarchic rebellion" (262). These two influences, Franklin maintains, have contributed to the present general character of American prison writing. Robert Gaucher sees a similar type of interaction in Canadian prison literature. He points out that the "relocation and redefinition of the convict and the prison also occurred in Canada in the 1960s, especially amongst its over-represented aboriginal minority" ("Inside Looking Out" 40). This development comes to be seen in prison literature: "In the prison writing of the 1960s and 1970s we see a coming together of the traditional collective perspective of oppressed minorities (Afro-Americans, Aboriginal Peoples), the Euro-American tradition of radical dissent and class struggle, and the prison focussed convict (as a subclass) perspective" ("Inside Looking Out" 40). Gaucher identifies three primary groups formed in the prison: the oppressed minority, the political detainee, and the prisoner as a (White) subclass. Like Franklin, but in a Canadian context, he emphasizes the joint impact of these perspectives in the formation of new prisoner consciousness and their mutual influence on the character of prison writing.

For many imprisoned writers, their writing often serves as a second hearing, an opportunity to intervene in their representation in the court and to expose the failings of the criminal justice system. *Stolen Life*, for instance, provides a sympathetic narrative medium for Yvonne Johnson to come forth with the testimony she does not give in court. Her personal history of racism, poverty, and abuse frames her hearing and informs the reader's perception of her later criminal involvement. Leonard Peltier and James Tyman similarly reconstruct their personal and cultural histories before calling on the reader to adjudicate. These three authors use their writing as a form of apology, defending their innocence, as Peltier does, or supplementing their conviction with personal details that were not permitted in their legal trials. In managing their texts in such a way, these writers manoeuvre around some of the constraints that the law places on self-representation. These narratives function, then, as an "alternative hearing"—as autobiography critic Leigh Gilmore calls it (145)—by allowing their authors to respond to the law's authority over their public and personal identities.

"To be a prisoner," Paul Gready observes, "is to be variously written" (493). Yet the prison can be the site of an unfolding literate self where the prison writer, laying claim to the cultural authority of narration, imagines an identity for him/herself apart from that of prisoner. Given the class politics of this writing and the disproportionate representation of the poor among those incarcerated, literacy is an important consideration for any study of prison literature. Correctional Services Canada estimates that 65 percent of individuals entering prison are functionally illiterate (Paul 19). As Brian Street argues in *Literacy in Theory and Practice*, literacy is not a "neutral technology" (65); to the contrary, it is steeped in ideological values and cannot be disentangled from its producers, the institutions it serves, and those who are denied it. It is interesting that many individuals discover that they are writers while in prison. As Judy Kalman observes in her study of adult literacy acquisition, those who become literate later in life may be led to question the logic of their former or ongoing marginality, and of the ideology that denied them literacy earlier in life. In many of the works featured in this book, the prison brings about a development in the prisoner that may allow him/her to escape the confinement of illiteracy. "Perhaps it is the intensity of the prison experience that demands a voice," Marianne Paul proposes in her guide to literacy programming in prison. "Perhaps it is the difficulty in maintaining an individual identity. The written word reinforces the fact that there is still an 'I'" (26).

The literature featured in this book has altered the perceptions of those who authored it; it also signifies an important recuperation of history. In *The Circle Game: Shadows and Substance in the Indian Residential School in Canada*, Roland Chrisjohn and Sherri Young note the dearth of historical accounts of the residential school: "When it comes to providing details of individuals' experiences in Residential School, or drawing generalizations about the form and function of the institution, there's [...] official silence. The churches and federal/provincial governments have produced no histories, incident reports, legal opinions, psychologies, or sociologies of Indian Residential Schooling. There is uniform inattention to these particular details" (27).

JanMohamed and Lloyd describe this inattention as an "institutional forgetting," a way of controlling the historical record while suppressing the collective memories of minority cultures (6). A recent explosion of residential school accounts by those who experienced these institutions has helped redress the ellipsis that Chrisjohn and Young identify. Crossing a variety of disciplines—history, literature, and therapy—these works perform a collective act of witnessing and enter various dialogues.

"Do social struggles give rise to new forms of literature?" asks John Beverley in his essay on the *testimonio* genre (91). Beverley's question directs critical attention to new genres formed out of different cultural and political contexts. At the centre of this book are writings that work from received literary forms such as poetry, the novel, and autobiography but that may also disrupt prevailing conceptions of literature in order to prioritize the social and cultural conditions that demand such articulations. An examination of the discursive character of this literature involves theorizing the relationship between content and genre. At times, the authors in this book rework existing forms; at other times, the choice of a given genre coincides with the experience about which the author writes. But while I am interested in the relation between form and the authors' institutional contexts, I try to avoid an unquestioning deference to Western literary classifications. Indeed, to assess the character of these writings in a way that yields to prevailing definitions of genre would be counterintuitive to much of the literature I explore. Critics of prison literature argue against the use of established literary approaches to understand this writing. "To comprehend the artistic achievement of this literature," Franklin proposes, "we must approach it with an aesthetic radically different from most aesthetics applied in the university and university-dominated cultural media" (235). Harlow similarly argues: "Reading prison writing must in turn demand a correspondingly activist counterapproach to that of passivity, aesthetic gratification, and the pleasures of consumption that are traditionally sanctioned by the academic disciplining of literature" (*Barred* 4). To write from the context of the prison is a significant act, an expression that represents more than matters of genre, form, and style can acknowledge.

Many of the texts featured in this book raise productive questions for literary studies, expanding and challenging taxonomies of literature, or changing the way this writing is received. A useful framework for examining this writing's overhauling of classificatory systems is Caren Kaplan's notion of "out-law genres"—writings that transgress or stretch literary boundaries to "uncover the power dynamics embedded in literary production, distribution, and reception" (119). Kaplan's attention to these literary innovations reminds us that the activity of theorizing genre is limited and that generic categories are "provisional and different in relation to specific struggles and locations" (125). Her coinage has a certain resonance with the texts I will explore—texts that reside on the margins of literary convention, and that furthermore, in the case of prison writing, literally come out of an "outlaw" space. A number of the works in this study challenge narrow configurations of genre or cross a variety of genres in the way that Kaplan describes. Yet how might this body of writing reframe Kaplan's theories? While Kaplan's use of "out-law" suggests writers who make legible their marginality through their writing, to what extent does her concept address incarcerated outlaw authors and their texts? What is the political and poetic imaginary of Kaplan's term, and how might the real, physical consignment of prisoners to the periphery of the public imagination and the social body challenge Kaplan's use of this metaphor? Incarcerated authors write from what is in many ways a place of radical difference. Such difference might caution against co-opting the trope of the outlaw or the metaphor of the imprisoned imagination.

Aims of Study

This investigation covers literary works written between 1971 and 1999. The earlier date coincides with the retraction of the White Paper, a significant turning point in Aboriginal peoples' relationship with the Canadian state. Following the example of Eisenhower's relocation policy (better known as Termination), Trudeau's White Paper proposed repealing the rights of Aboriginal people guaranteed in the Indian Act and in individual treaties. This policy would have terminated the legal distinction between Aboriginal people and other Canadians. Aboriginal groups in Canada who witnessed the impact of Termination in the United States recognized the odious agenda behind this legislation. The National Indian Brotherhood declared that the White Paper would be "the destruction of a nation of people" (in McFarlane 109). Harold Cardinal, one of the leaders of the indigenous rights movement in Canada, responded by publishing *The Unjust Society: The Tragedy of Canada's Indians*. That book described to the Canadian public in an unprecedented way the social and political situation of this country's indigenous people. Numerous Aboriginal-run small newspapers ran articles and editorial cartoons denouncing the proposed legislation. The collective response of Aboriginal people was vigorous enough to block the legislation's passage. The White Paper, paradoxically, brought together First Nations in an unpredicted way. Aboriginal people's mobilization at this political juncture occurred in tandem with the rise of the American Indian Movement and the 1971 publication of *Bury My Heart at Wounded Knee*, a work that chronicled the displacement and genocide of indigenous people in North America. Two years earlier, Kiowa author N. Scott Momaday had won the Pulitzer Prize for his novel *House Made of Dawn*. Momaday's work, which followed the struggle of its Tano protagonist to live in a world divided between two cultures, inspired many later authors and launched a renaissance in indigenous writing in the United States and Canada.

Given these dialogues across Indian Country, the appearance of indigenous authors writing in the United States will come as little surprise in this study. Leonard Peltier's autobiography, a touchstone work for this examination, figures at various points alongside the writing of imprisoned indigenous authors in Canada. Peltier's flight to and subsequent extradition from Canada following the Pine Ridge shooting for which he would later stand accused place part of his story in this country. The Assembly of First Nations' involvement in Peltier's campaigns for release further reinforces Peltier's symbolic power for Aboriginal people in Canada. Kanien'keheka songwriter and musician Robbie Robertson, who collaborated with Peltier on his 1998 album, describes Peltier as "a hero in the First Nations community" (Bliss). Peltier's story is especially resonant for the writers featured in this study, writers who, if not imprisoned themselves, are mindful of their checked freedoms.

Part One of this book looks at the use of genre in the institutional setting of the prison. These works span a number of genres ranging from autobiography, memoir, and collaborative life writing to poetry, essays, and oral forms. In my consideration of these texts, I seek out the relation between the author's prison setting and the modes of writing in which s/he engages. In what ways do these writers adapt literary and oral forms to their specific context? How do they manage their writing to structure a separate hearing? What rhetorical and discursive modes—for instance, apology, confession, testimony—do the authors deploy? What audience does this writing envisage?

An underlying consideration throughout the first half of this book is the stance of the prison writer, the role the author constructs in relation to his/her imagined community. In many of the texts discussed, the authors insist that they are typical—that is, representative of a larger cultural group. How does the choice of a life-writing genre enable this articulation of a collective identity? As I move from Peltier and Tyman, who claim to speak on behalf of a unified indigenous collective, to Yvonne Johnson and other female prisoner authors, I trouble this assumption of "representativeness." Johnson's writing points to certain challenges in claiming a representative role and to the multiple configurations of identity that may result instead. Some authors construct more practical, contingent communities. These authors put forth a type of identity that is situational and mutable, the product of different immediate contexts such as the institution of the prison. The basis of a grouping may be gender, as many of the works by Aboriginal female inmates demonstrate. Although this book proceeds from a recognition of the shared, unique relationship of Aboriginal peoples to carceral institutions in this country, it also explores the formations of sub-communities that expand or move in satellites around a collective Aboriginal identity.

Part Two turns to the use of genre in residential school narratives. The narrators featured in this part of my discussion assert a degree of self-determination over their developing identities, an independent consciousness that defies the residential school's control. What is the relation between genre and content in these texts? To what extent do these authors conform to or interrogate the conventions of the genres they engage? I consider these questions alongside Basil Johnston's residential school memoir, *Indian School Days*, Tomson Highway's semi-autobiographical novel, *Kiss of the Fur Queen*, Rita Joe's autobiographical poems about residential schooling, "Hated Structure" and "I Lost My Talk," and Jane Willis's residential school autobiography, *Geniesh: An Indian Girlhood*.

Taken as a whole, this book investigates the cultural importance of carceral institutions in Aboriginal literature and history. While the general aim of my project is to channel attention to a neglected area of study and to highlight the formal, critical, and aesthetic implications of this literature, it seeks not just the recovery of these works as literature but an awareness of the ethical and epistemological questions that accompany the reading of these texts. The reading strategies employed in this book emphasize, to a far greater degree, the discursive strategies employed by the authors and the social as well as literary consequence of this literature.

Why does prison writing matter? Franklin points out that in the United States, the growing criminalization of dissent, the rising numbers of traffic and criminal offences, and the increase in mechanisms of surveillance are closing the gap between "the criminal prisoner-author and the law-abiding citizen-reader" (242). In Franklin's thinking, the barriers between historically imprisoned groups and privileged ones are beginning to break down. At the end of his work he posits the prisoner as an important symbol of class oppression and of the erosion of individual freedoms: "This consciousness [...] has now transcended the experiences of one people. [...] It has broken through to a class perception of U.S. social reality, and hence has deeply influenced not only white inmates but much of the white populace" (247–48). In Franklin's thinking, the prisoner has begun to reflect a non-imprisoned public's imperilled social freedoms, as well as the economic and class factors that come into play in criminalization and detention. The prisoner emerges as an important domestic voice, a reminder of internal social ills and of the vulnerability of the individual to the state's repressive strategies. A saying used to circulate in a British Columbia penitentiary: "See that guy over there? That's me. If you don't believe me, go and ask him. But don't be surprised if he says he's you" (Guiney 7).

Whatever the reminders about the prisoner's significance to a dominant public, Robert Gaucher points to a recent public antipathy toward prisoners in Canada. As evidence of the negative attention that prisoners generate, Gaucher cites the proposed federal legislation, Bill C-220 (1997), known as the Son of Sam bill. Modelled after existing legislation in the United States and Australia banning the publication of accounts detailing convicted authors' crimes,[3] this bill was promoted in Canada with the idea of preventing criminals from telling their "lurid tales" (Marowits). Under this law, the copyright and profits of a work recounting an incarcerated author's crime would have been subject to seizure by the Crown. "The precipitating moral panic" behind this move for censorship, Gaucher points out, was incited by "the public and political involvement of the organized and punitively oriented crime victims lobby in Canada" ("Inside Looking Out" 42). He explains: "During the considerations of this bill by the Canadian House of Commons, *the only type* of prison writing mentioned and considered by Members of Parliament and during testimony to the House Committee (supposedly) studying the matter, was 'true crime' depictions of the 'gory details' of 'heinous criminal acts'" (42; emphasis Gaucher's). These discussions promoted a narrow view of both the prisoner and prisoner-author. The bill passed unanimously in the House of Commons before it was blocked by the Senate. Legislation similar to Bill C-220 passed in Ontario in 2002 and came into effect on July 1, 2003. Under Ontario's Prohibiting Profiting from Recounting Crimes Act (formerly Bill 69), the profits of a work published by an incarcerated author are to be seized and held in trust for victims to claim. Copyright, however, remains with the author. In contrast to Franklin's arguments of the prisoner's growing importance to a wider public audience, this legislation reflects a prejudicial view of prisoners. Such representations reveal a public sensitivity based not on identification but on fear.

In February 1998, Rudy Wiebe testified before the Senate against Bill C-220, reading aloud a letter by Yvonne Johnson in which she explained her reasons for writing and correcting sensationalist impressions of inmates. Wiebe prefaced his case by pointing out that "writing in prison has been a time-honored way through which many prisoners have found their own redemption. In so doing, some have made most significant contributions to literature and society's knowledge of its own frailties and failures" (Canada, Parliament). Wiebe went on to suggest the possible affinities between inmates in Canada and political prisoners abroad. He underlined the crucial role that written accounts about or by prisoners have played in the release of individuals such as Guy Paul Morin, Donald Marshall, and

David Milgaard. He then quoted from Johnson's letter, in which she affirmed the importance of her and Wiebe's literary undertaking: "I did not write my book to glamorize my offence in any way. An RCMP officer suggested I write a book so that others may learn from my mistakes and hopefully not follow my footsteps. [...] I have been silenced by my abuse over the years, however, the process of writing has helped me to break that painful spell. If Bill C-220 were in effect, I would suffer in silence forever, along with other people who might heal through this avenue" (ibid.).

Here, Johnson was underscoring the therapeutic function of writing. "This book is a visible healing process that has helped me gather better understanding, and learning," she further attested (ibid.). She then proceeded to present herself as a voice of all prisoners: "I stand as a person on behalf of all people incarcerated in Canada, encouraging you to empathize with how Bill C-220 will directly affect all of us" (ibid.). Johnson moved from emphasizing the personal and instructive value of her text to instilling the universal importance of writing as an outlet and recourse for all inmates.

A self-critical question has occurred to me at various points during this project: Does this book's emphasis on the prison as a central, structuring presence in First Nations writing focus too exclusively on a negative aspect of Aboriginal history? I recall Alan Velie's statement: "White Americans, whether sympathetic or not to Indian concerns, tend to view Indian history in tragic or ironic terms, thinking primarily in terms of Indian failures and disasters" (198–99). Though Velie refers to White collaborators who colour Aboriginal accounts with their own outlook on the plight of indigenous people, his statement applies also to critics whose selection of information can suggest a certain narrative. My work focuses, however, on the innovative ways in which indigenous people have managed to maintain their sense of sovereignty and solidarity where these have been eroded by the law. The authors who appear in this examination use their writing as form of defence, as a therapeutic mechanism, and as a site of community formation. At times this literature also contributes to the reworking and preservation of indigenous traditions. The type of critical inquiry represented by this book, I am convinced, is important and worthwhile.

Although this study identifies a discrete corpus of literature dealing with the theme of imprisonment from the perspective of Aboriginal authors, it hopes to reinforce the significance of these texts to Canadian literary and critical discussions. While urging that Aboriginal literature be recognized as its own site of cultural and literary production, this examination also attempts to bring this body of writing into dialogue with a national literary consciousness. My position is that indigenous authors writing about the insidious experience of incarceration in post-contact Aboriginal life have a crucial place in literary cultures other than their own—that such texts, in Emma LaRocque's words, hold up "powerful mirrors to Canadian society" (xviii). As the epigraph to the collection of prison writing, *Native Sons*, reads: "We speak / because / you need / to understand" (Batisse n.p.). The recognition of these largely occluded accounts by various reading communities is a crucial step in producing the dialogue this writing seeks.

Notes

1 Marshall's story is chronicled in Michael Harris's *Justice Denied: The Law Versus Donald Marshall*, though the accuracy of Harris's recreation of the murder was called into doubt after the Royal Commission hearings. For further reading on the Royal Commission on the Donald Marshall, Jr. Prosecution, see the collection, *Elusive Justice: Beyond the Donald Marshall Inquiry*, edited by Joy Mannette. That the Royal Commission hearings did not sufficiently challenge juridical process is one of the points on which critics have faulted the Marshall Inquiry. While the commission represented an alternative forum for seeking justice, its structure and outcome did not, M.E. Turpel argues, question the prevailing judicial model, nor did it "consider what kind of justice system Aboriginal peoples could respect" (92). Rather, as Mannette contends, the Royal Commission served to "allay public doubt about judicial process, state legal coherence, and administrative rationality" (65). The inquiry promoted a kind of soft justice, as it were, culminating in a trial "in which no one goes to jail" (Salter 2). The Commission's inaction with regard to the laying of criminal charges against police officials who suppressed evidence and obstructed justice is another disappointment some have identified with the inquiry and report.
2 Anthony Hall points out, using the example of Aboriginal people in Canada, that the Fourth World might be seen as failing to account for "the uneasy state of relations between Aboriginal elites and the most marginalized citizens" such as "the homeless urban poor, the victims of domestic violence and child abuse, the physically disabled or the mentally ill, the drug addicted, the recurringly incarcerated, the gays and lesbians, and various associations of women" (285). These internally marginalized groups, Hall observes, have been largely silenced within top-down structures of Aboriginal governance.
3 This legislation, as it was proposed, would have applied to individuals who have been indicted for violent offences and sentenced to a minimum of five years.

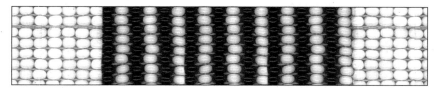

PART ONE **Genre in the Institutional Setting of the Prison**

Prison literature occupies a curious, one might even say paradoxical, place in a society's philosophical and literary imagination. In his introduction to *The Time Gatherers*, a collection of prisoners' writing, Hugh MacLennan summarizes the attraction of prison writing for non-incarcerated readers: "If other readers are like myself, they will find some pages here which will make them see things they never saw before" (4). With its putative ability to make visible what is hidden from public view—to approximate the world of an abject other—the writing of incarcerated subjects represents that part of the social body that has been denied, the "excess" that has been cast aside. It would be a simplification, however, to regard prison literature as a mere sore on the social body. Many leaders, influential thinkers, and celebrated artists were at one point incarcerated: Moses, Jesus, Bunyan, Cervantes, Dostoevsky, Wilde, Gramsci, Gandhi, Billie Holiday, and Nelson Mandela are but a diverse few. Indeed, the prison experience is an archetypal one of both heroes and outcasts. Poet, critic, and former prisoner Michael Hogan makes a further argument that the prison is a metaphor for society itself, a microcosm of the benevolent state's absolute albeit often unperceivable control of its citizens. "Barely discernible to the person who is not on parole and has no criminal record," this power, Hogan notes, is most intelligible to the prisoner, whose unique vantage point allows him to see the world differently, often with a "jaundiced" eye (89–90).

A long-standing site of writing, the prison also produces authors who may not otherwise have been moved to write. More than a place of defeat and submission, the prison may be seen as a place of learning, where a nascent consciousness is born in the prisoner, often in defiant resistance to the institution containing him/her. Consider the following lines written by an Aboriginal female prisoner, Elaine Antone:

> [...] my mind
> A devious, fool proof scheme
> Keys can't lock away my thoughts.
>
> Key pushers, keys turn in their locks
> Reform me!! (n.p.)

The speaker continues by addressing the prison administration: "Reform me as I grow from 17 to 18 to 19, to 20, / A child, my age 18, you say, "belongs in school" (n.p.).

"Has it ever once occurred to you," she asks, "That, that is exactly where I am!" "In here I learn the con games, sad games, / Yes, within this prison ... I learn ..." (n.p.). Leonard Peltier echoes Antone's characterization of the prison when he remarks that "prison's the only university, the only finishing school many young Indian brothers ever see" (67). Part of this "schooling" is criminal, as the speaker of the above poem implies; it involves learning how to "slip and slide," as it is called in prison lingo—that is, to survive the games of the prison. Along with this admission of deviance, however, is an insistence on a type of enlightenment that occurs in this place. A 1976 issue of *Tightwire*, a magazine published from Kingston's Prison for Women, features a cartoon of a female prisoner in a meeting with "A.D. Ministration." The administrator's balloon reads: "Yes 001, we are prepared to acknowledge that since you've been here you've won the Nobel Peace Prize, found a cure for cancer, solved the riddle of the universe, [...] solved the problem of world starvation, developed a non-polluting fuel, invented an anti-gravity device, developed an interplanetary communications system, and instituted a revolutionary method where by [sic] the deaf can hear, the blind can see and the dumb can speak ... But we still think that you are devious, manipulative, and a threat to society!" ("Cartoon" 41).

Some prisoners view their potential to contribute to society from prison as significant, though misunderstood. While such talents may be wasted by the idleness of serving prison time, there is an opportunity for self-discovery and creative output within this space. Writing is part of this introspective process. "'Who am I? Why do I do these things?'" asks Gregory McMaster, an incarcerated writer serving a life sentence at Collins Bay. "Try as they might," he writes, "there is not a single correctional program that can supply the answers to these questions. The truth lays buried deep within us and writing is the tool we use to peel away the layers" (46).

Writing is not the only recourse to healing. Some Aboriginal prisoners, Yvonne Johnson for example, reconnect with their cultural origins and spiritual traditions while in prison. The emergence of Native Brotherhood and Sisterhood groups was instrumental in developing an active political voice within Canadian prisons, one that saw the prisoner increasingly in ideological terms. These groups, along with Native-run prison publications dating back to the 1960s, demonstrate an active engagement with social and political movements outside the prison walls.

These examples lend support to the view that the vectors of influence between the prison and outside society are two-way. Prison discourse and thinking permeate outside language and thought in ways that are often indiscernible. Joseph Bruchac makes a similar case when he defends the significance of prison poetry and points out that the "majority society is continually absorbing (in small doses) words and phrases which originate in the constantly changing body of prison slang" ("Breaking Out" 287). Bruchac's point that prison lexicon infiltrates outside discourses serves as evidence that the discursive developments within the prison are not bound by their walls.

Prison literature is, by its very site of creation, polemical: it defies the disciplinary structures that attempt to suppress it. Many of the texts emerging from prisons challenge the taxonomy and definition of literature as they have been established in the West. Writing by Aboriginal inmates is doubly marginalized, fighting off presumptions of who can write, grappling with the erasure that the law has exacted and that the literary establishment has aided and abetted. With this insurgent body of prison writing, the question is not simply "how the incarcerated imagination has become part of Western ideas and literature" (Davies 7) but how these "out-law" texts speak back, reinscribing rather than reifying the generic codes that underpin Western literary traditions. How do these authors enable genre to speak against a silence that judicial and legal institutions have forced upon them? What new critical vocabularies do these texts generate, and how can academic study address this literature in a way that accentuates rather than neutralizes its political statements?

The first half of this book takes up these questions in relation to a diverse sample of writing from prison. Two underlying considerations follow this analysis. The first relates to the discursive character of these texts—that is, how these authors use and rework received forms. A second focus is how the social context of the prison imprints itself on this writing. I will look, then, at the discursive strategies engaged by the writers while also exploring these texts as windows into a local culture.

My discussion begins with an examination of Leonard Peltier's *Prison Writings*. Probably the most widely known Native person serving prison time, Peltier is a spectral figure in much of the writing by Aboriginal inmates. Yet his text does not focus on the evolving life of the individual subject. Peltier disavows any sense of himself as exceptional or exemplary. "You must understand ... I am ordinary. Painfully ordinary," Peltier tells us, having just pronounced that "*all* of my people are suffering, so I'm in no way special in that regard" (9). He identifies himself as part of a collective body; thus, his incarceration stands in for the ideological, systemic, and physical oppression of Aboriginal people. He reflects on the intersection between his experience and those of indigenous people on this continent: "My own personal story can't be told, even in this abbreviated version, without going back long before my own birth on September 12, 1944, back to 1890 and to 1876 and to 1868 and to 1851 and, yes, all the way back through all the other calamitous dates in the relations between red men and white" (50). His story collapses into a larger history to reveal a notion of self that is in metonymic relation to that of an entire people. "I'm a small part of a much larger story," he insists. "My autobiography is the story of my people [...] My life has meaning only in relation to them" (43). Peltier's personal testimony is what Brian Swann terms "historic witness," a type of writing "that grows out of a past that is very much a present" (xvii).[1]

Some key differences, however, set Peltier apart from the other authors in this discussion. Peltier was already an activist when he was arrested. He did not depend on going to prison to know himself as Native; in fact, he went to prison *because of* his commitment to a political and cultural cause. Peltier's emergence in *Prison Writings* as a voice for his people is a subject position we also see at the end of James Tyman's autobiography. However, Tyman's imprisonment lacks the political and collective significance of Peltier's. Peltier declares himself wrongfully imprisoned, and moreover, a "political prisoner"; by contrast, Tyman admits that many of his crimes were gratuitous. Tyman and Yvonne Johnson are in prison for crimes that are not in any local sense "political." Both lacked strong community ties prior to their imprisonment. Tyman's view of himself as part of a collective body is only incipiently developed in the latter pages of his text. Unlike Peltier, he deals little with the collective history of Aboriginal people, keeping his focus on his own life until a brief movement outward at the end of his work. The representative role he assumes, I will argue, appears to be vital to his own evolving identity rather than to the larger collective on whose behalf he claims to speak. His self-positioning as a spokesperson for indigenous people resolves the sense of alienation and displacement detailed in much of his autobiography.

Tyman's work blends together a true-crime narrative with autobiography. This mode of writing makes for a more conventional and in some ways predictable prison text, one that is also less experimental in form than *Prison Writings* and *Stolen Life*. Like Tyman's autobiography, *Stolen Life* devotes a great deal of the narrative to Johnson's experiences of racism, poverty, sexual abuse, and mistreatment by the law—circumstances that soften her criminal image and draw attention away from her participation in a murder. Johnson's development is similar to Tyman's in that she transcends her individual isolation and sees herself as part of a collective. Both *Inside Out* and *Stolen Life* end with their authors achieving a sense of reconciliation with their Aboriginal identities and, moreover, extending their sense of identification outward in their appeals to a non-Native readership. Yet Johnson and Wiebe engage various forms and discursive modes to produce a self-conscious, collaborative work. Their managing of genre becomes a site of meaning in itself. Collaborative auto/biography allows Johnson an opportunity for self-representation that she forfeits in a judicial context. My discussion of *Stolen Life* will focus on the limits the law places on Johnson as a testifying subject and on the sympathetic narrative vehicle this text provides for her to come forth with her account. Testimony, witnessing, confession—these discursive modes will come into play in my analysis of the different rhetorical registers of *Stolen Life*. Together, these multiple discursive registers create a context for Johnson's appeal.

Following my discussion of these three autobiographical works, I will sample writing from *Tightwire*, a magazine published from Kingston's Prison for Women; *Words from Inside*, an annual collection published by the Prison Arts Foundation; and *Native Sons*, a 1977 collection by prisoners at the Guelph Correctional Centre. The works from these publications show the "temper and feel" (Gaucher, "Canadian Penal Press" 5) of writing emerging from prisons. My investigation will explore the different literary modes these authors take up to write about their prison experiences and the types of readership they envision. Unfortunately, what is most striking about some of this writing is lost in my reproduction of it here— that is, its material, tangible connection to its place of creation. Many of the writings published in internal "joint" magazines like *Tightwire* did not have the advantage of good, or even any, editing—unless one includes, of course, the defacement of the institutional magic marker censoring their content. Arguably, what makes this writing inferior by some standards also makes it direct and intensified by others. There is, as Joseph Bruchac writes, a "special energy" in this "community of letters" ("Breaking Out" 294), a charged element that distinguishes this socially engaged literature.

Note

1 Although Brian Swann uses this term to describe American indigenous poetry, it usefully describes the role of collective memory in Peltier's *Prison Writings*.

ONE Barred Subject
Leonard Peltier's
Prison Writings

Leonard Peltier's *Prison Writings* provides a recent, paradigmatic example of the generic innovation and reinscription of master discourses from the prison. Convicted of killing two FBI officers on the Pine Ridge Reservation in South Dakota on June 26, 1975, Peltier is sitting out two life sentences in Leavenworth Federal Penitentiary in Kansas. His story is one of international magnitude, invoked by many as representative of the American government's violation of human rights and of its use of the criminal justice system to neutralize dissent. The events that precipitated Peltier's involvement at Pine Ridge speak to a historical struggle of indigenous people to rise above poverty, deracination, and political disenfranchisement.

In 1973 the American Indian Movement (AIM) carried out a seventy-one-day siege of Wounded Knee on the Pine Ridge Lakota Reservation. Coupled with their occupation of the BIA (Bureau of Indian Affairs) in Washington, D.C., a few months earlier, the siege drew public attention toward an intractable and potentially militant response by American indigenous people to unsatisfactory living conditions, expropriated land and resources, and unheard petitions for public reparations.

The two years leading up to the shootout in which Peltier was allegedly involved were an intensely violent period on the Pine Ridge Reservation.

Several unsolved deaths and beatings occurred between 1973 and 1975. It is suspected that the "reign of terror" waged by tribal leader Dick Wilson and his group of thugs dubbed the GOONs (Guardians of the Oglala Nation) had the backing of the FBI and the BIA. The residents who were being terrorized opposed Wilson's leadership, claiming that it was guided by self-interest and was worsening living conditions on the reservation. Pine Ridge was kept under close watch during this period. The area had the greatest number of FBI agents per capita in the United States—a buildup that reached its height six days before the murders for which Peltier was convicted.

During this volatile time, members of AIM—Peltier among them— were invited to Pine Ridge by the Traditional Elders of the Oglala Lakota to protect the imperilled residents. On June 26 an unmarked car driven by two FBI agents trailed a vehicle onto the reservation, supposedly in pursuit of individuals suspected of stealing a pair of cowboy boots. The threat that an unmarked vehicle represented was well understood by the local people. Paul Berg, a former BIA employee who worked for the FBI on Pine Ridge during the siege, recalls the intimidation tactics that were used: "The FBI had a habit of stopping their cars on reservation roads and aiming their M-16s at approaching vehicles. Since FBI cars were unmarked, people approaching in an oncoming vehicle would frequently panic and flee. The agents would pursue and apprehend the fleeing vehicle."[1] What happened next is consistent with Berg's description. The individuals pursued by the unmarked car apparently assumed they were in danger. A shootout began that left the two FBI agents and one Aboriginal man dead. The death of the Aboriginal man was not investigated; but the authorities conducted a dragnet throughout the surrounding territory to find those who had shot the FBI agents. In the belief that he would be targeted because of his unfavourable record with the FBI, Peltier fled to Canada. Within eight months he was extradited on the basis of a witness named Myrtle Poor Bear, who later claimed she had been coerced into signing an affidavit stating, falsely, that Peltier had been present at the crime scene. In what some have declared a miscarriage of justice, Peltier was convicted of both murders in 1977.

Given the political circumstances of his imprisonment, Peltier's text immediately suggests an altogether different writing enterprise than strictly an individualized self-study. *Prison Writings* calls on typical features of the prison autobiography in its apologetic stance and theology of the afterlife. However, Peltier's apology is a defence of his people's actions, and the theology he invokes overturns Judeo-Christian concepts in favour of his own Anishnabe and Lakota cosmologies. Autobiography, in Peltier's handling, becomes both a public rebuttal and an intimate self-reflection—

a medium for disrupting the authority of legal and Christian discourse while simultaneously exploring the development of his consciousness from within a "stone-and-steel hole" (xxvi).

From the very foreword of the text, Peltier sets out to critique the system that incarcerated him by challenging the principles it purports to uphold. "Innocence is the weakest defence," he begins, thus establishing his guiltlessness as well as his defencelessness (xxiii). With this pre-emptive plea, he then begins to undermine the judicial process and the status of truth within it. "Innocence is a single voice that can only say over and over again, 'I didn't do it,'" he reasons, whereas "guilt has a thousand voices, all of them lies" (xxiii). His pleas exhausted, he then ceases to address the system vitiating his testimony. "I have pleaded my innocence for so long now, in so many courts of law, in so many public statements," he submits, "that I will not argue it here" (xxiii). He will later reinforce the same intent by insisting that "this book is not a plea or a justification. Neither is it an explanation or an apology for the events that overtook my life and many other lives in 1975" (9). With this, Peltier intends to turn away from an apologia, or a formal defence of his actions. Insofar as he has done so, he has created the grounds for an "alternative hearing," one that will frame his testimony by rejecting the official discourse of state justice. Writing becomes his means of self-representation, an opportunity for him to forge an identity apart from the one overdetermined by the law.

Peltier's testimony evades the constraints that the law places on self-representation. He offers his account outside a legalistic framework in order to promote, in Leigh Gilmore's words, an "alternative jurisprudence" (44). I want to hover for a moment over this notion of an "alternative jurisprudence" in order to consider its broader cultural implications. Many Aboriginal communities are regaining jurisdiction over the treatment of offenders and are returning to traditional, community-based methods of restorative justice.[2] "Justice," Patricia Monture-Angus notes, is a word that has no direct equivalent in some indigenous languages (such as Blackfoot, Musquem [Salish], and Kanien'keheka [Mohawk]).[3] In the Anishnabe language, the closest equivalent is *ti-baq-nee-qwa-win*, which literally means "to come before a system for something that has already been done wrong" (238). Monture-Angus interprets this reference to a "system" as a reference to a Euro-American system of law. The Anishnabe word for "justice," then, is possibly a post-contact term, the product of a colonial relationship. Justice carries with it a historical "residue," to borrow Wai Chee Dimock's term; thus it is ensconced in a set of relations in which it can only prevail.

Peltier transvalues the notion of testimony by altering the context in and conditions from which it is offered. "What follows in these pages, then," Peltier self-reflexively establishes, "is my own personal testament as best I can set it down under the circumstances" (xxv). Testimony, in Peltier's usage, suggests the exploration of his political and spiritual consciousness through the journal entries, political reflections, and poetry assembled within his text. But this description of his writing as a "personal testament" also invokes a sense of legality. He appears to turn away from the system that sentenced him, yet he continues to address it in his writing. Indeed, this work is, among many other things, a repudiation of his guilt and an amassing of reflections that will be used in his defence.

The imperative of setting the record straight appears throughout this text, most notably in the final appendix, in which Peltier reproduces his 1977 presentencing statement. This appendix serves as a platform for Peltier to redress the injustices he faced throughout his Fargo trial and in the legal hearings that followed. The manufacturing of evidence, coercion of witnesses, and abuse of authority that he maintains led to his conviction serve as a premise for Peltier's critique of Euro-American notions of justice. Peltier denounces the Western legal system by enumerating its inequities and failings. He recalls the judge's words to him: "*You profess to be an activist for your people, but you are a disservice to Native Americans*'" (237; italics in original). By appropriating the judge's words, Peltier inflects them with his discordantly different perspective. He intervenes in the record of that day by reversing the flow of dialogue and, by extension, the flow of representation. As a rebuttal to the judge's estimation of his character, Peltier offers his presentencing statement. He prefaces this statement by declaring to the reader, "*I will let you—and history—decide who spoke the truth that dark day in the history of American injustice*" (237; italics in original). Peltier here is calling on the reader to adjudicate. Despite his claim to the contrary in the foreword, this work cannot help returning to his innocence, to a defence of his actions leading up to his imprisonment, and to the indelible imprint his prison sentence has left on his life narrative. The entire text, including the introduction, the preface, and the appendices, inevitably circles back to Peltier's claim of innocence.

Peltier's writing is concerned with history, and his rationalization of his actions becomes a rationalization of his people's resistance to oppression in the years leading up to his life story. The prologue to Peltier's life is the criminalized political resistance and loss of sovereignty that his Anishnabe and Lakota ancestors experienced. The Seventh Cavalry's 1890 massacre of more than two hundred Lakota Sioux at Wounded Knee epitomizes the repeated blows against this nation's fight for dignity and survival. Peltier rebuts the historical representation of this event as a heroic victory. His discussion of the massacre seeks to adjust historical accounts of this event while also showing its bearing on the present. "These atrocities against my people continue to this day," he maintains, "only now they're carried out with more sophisticated means than Gatling guns and cannons and sabers. There are subtler means of killing" (54).

During his lifetime, Peltier witnessed his home community endure similar blows at an economic level. As a child growing up on the Turtle Mountain (Anishnabe) Reservation, Peltier watched his community suffer under further government manoeuvring with its 1952 Federal Relocation Policy. Also known as Termination, this legislation cut off a great deal of money and support to indigenous groups, including treaty rights. Promoted as a way of fostering self-determination among indigenous people in the United States, the legislation exacerbated the existing poverty of many tribal peoples by reclaiming huge expanses of territory for industry and non-Aboriginal enterprises. Michael Dorris interprets the motivations behind this policy: "It talked of giving Indians 'equal rights' and of 'freeing them from federal support and control and from all the disabilities and limitations specifically applicable to Indians'—as if no one realized that in equalizing rights, Indians were forfeiting those very advantages for which their ancestors had exchanged most of North America" (188–89). Extreme poverty, geographical displacement, and cultural disbanding befell the 109 indigenous nations affected by this policy, who were left with little choice but to move to cities or continue starving on reservations. Although this legislation affected American indigenous people specifically, parallels exist between the termination act and Canada's 1969 White Paper. Similarly promoted as an enabling initiative for Native people, this proposal, Olive Dickason points out, was a response to AIM's growing influence in Canada. The White Paper was as controversial as the termination policy in the United States, and it drew similar opposition from Aboriginal groups until it was retracted in 1971.

Peltier uses his writing as a way to testify not only against his individual experience of injustice but also against the injustices suffered by his cultural community. As he exposes the government and legal rhetoric that has misrepresented him, he draws attention to the larger consequences this same rhetoric has had in the lives of his people. For instance, he provides his personal experiences with the relocation policies of the Eisenhower administration: "A resolution was passed by Congress and signed by President Eisenhower to 'terminate' all Indian reservations and to 'relocate' us off our lands and into the cities. Those suddenly became the most important, the most feared, words in our vocabulary: 'termination' and 'relocation.' I can think of few words more sinister in the English language, at least to Indian people [...] To us, those words were an assault on our very existence as a people, an attempt to eradicate us" (80).

Peltier comments on the toxic effects this terminology has for those whose lives have been affected by such policies. And he takes a similar approach to exposing the FBI's organized campaign against activists like himself: "We were, quite simply, in the FBI's own choice phrase, to be 'neutralized'" (107). The same power that has sought to "eradicate" Peltier as an activist has also attempted to eradicate his people and their sovereignty. A point of convergence between Peltier's individual past and this collective history, then, is this shared relationship to official state discourse. Like the historical treatment of his people, his individual persecution has run up against the same rhetoric. In this way Peltier sets up a continuum in which all his life experiences are representative of indigenous people.

In much the same way that he reinflects and sharply denounces the language of the legal state, Peltier critiques Judeo-Christian concepts. He strongly equates prison with hell. Consider this description of his entry into Leavenworth:

> I walked in my shackles and leg-irons up the front steps to the first of a seemingly endless series of steel doors. I thought I could hear distant screams coming from somewhere within the building. [...] When I turned to one of the marshals who was leading me up the stairs, hoping to find some glint of human warmth in his eyes, I saw, instead, not a face at all, but a mask of absolute hatred and a look in his eyes so vile that it can't even be described. [...] He just smiled a devil's smile and said in an almost cheerful voice, "You're dead, you fucking Indian bastard, you'll never get out of this building alive." (155–56)

As Peltier enters the prison, he joins what he perceives to be the ghosts of tortured souls. His passage is heralded by a spiritless marshal whose stone countenance turns to gall as he considers pleading with him for his soul. The marshal's poisonous response is more than an expression of racial acrimony: Peltier is denied grace as a "fucking Indian bastard." The damnation continues as the marshal's face and head "turn into a serpent's, spitting its venom at me" (156). The allusion to hell is explicit several pages later when Peltier refers to himself as "a houseguest in hell" in one of the devil's "many mansions" (158).

Peltier turns his attention to inflecting and subverting the official discourses that have branded him guilty. One of the master discourses he overwrites is Christian doctrine. In a poem titled "Aboriginal Sin," he points out the original guilt of Aboriginal people under Christianity:

> *We Indians are all guilty,*
> *guilty of being ourselves.*

We're taught that guilt from the day we're born.
We learn it well. (16; italics Peltier's)

This poem develops Peltier's disidentification with Christian doctrine. Under this belief system he can never be innocent—a state not unlike his immovable verdict of guilt within the justice system. "Aboriginal sin" implies an inborn guilt, a guilt that is racially designated. In the paradoxical assertion, *"Your guilt makes you holy"* (16), Peltier undermines Christian principles by inverting its meanings. He reads new meaning into the Christian notion of original sin by replacing guilt with vindication, a type of immunity from this belief system. At the same time, he turns this language against those who have wronged him. He asks the federal authorities responsible for his indictment: "I often wonder what fitful dreams come to them at night if they truly believe in their Christian God and the eternal sizzling hell that surely lies waiting for them" (18–19). He maintains a distance from this belief system; even so, he deploys Christian discourse as a rhetorical weapon and mobilizes its concepts to expose its contradictions.

The Christian discourse Peltier subverts is linked to the legal and judicial institutions he contests. He draws attention to the Christian underpinnings of American legal and governing institutions as he indicts the "white racist American Establishment, which consistently said 'In God We Trust' while they went about the business of murdering my people and attempting to destroy our culture" (242). One of the angles, then, from which he attacks the American legal, juridical, and governing institutions regulating these injustices is their Christian foundations. Religious and legal discourses converge in Peltier's writing. His description of his legal punishment, his imprisonment, as a hell is a primary instance of the proximity suggested between these two systems. Peltier's text reflects a tradition encountered in many prison writings—the invocation of the afterlife. But Peltier goes beyond this typical feature of prison texts by inserting his own indigenous spiritual practices in place of a Christian cosmology or conversion. These alternative spiritual rituals enable him to transcend the physical space of the prison. At the same time, they offer a way out of the Christian hell to which he has been sentenced.

Peltier rejects Christian theology as a means to assert the primacy of indigenous spiritual beliefs. The conversion he depicts in *Prison Writings* represents his journey toward an appreciation of indigenous sacred knowledge. Two indigenous rituals figure in his text: the Sun Dance and the *inipi*, or sweat. The Sun Dance, he explains, is a feat of discipline, a means to ascend to lucidity through the overcoming of one's physical state: "There is a separation, a detachment, a greater mind that you become part of, so that you both feel the pain and see yourself feeling the pain. And then, somehow, the pain becomes contained, limited [...] The pain explodes into a bright white light, into revelation" (11).

The Sun Dance allows Peltier to reconceive of his time in prison as a spiritual exercise. In somewhat similar fashion, the Anishnabe sweat lodge ceremony "makes each Saturday morning holy here in the otherwise unholy Leavenworth" (183). The *inipi* offers transcendence and revelation:

> Sitting there naked in the superheated darkness, your bare knees only inches from the molten rocks in the central pit, you come right up against the cutting edge of your own fear, your own pain [...] And yet, in that fear, when you face it eye to eye, there's an *awareness* ...
>
> If nothing else, it begins as an awareness of the fear itself. And then, somehow, you pass right through fear, right through that pain. (185–86)

Like the Sun Dance, the sweat allows Peltier to transcend his physical limitations, even his physical self. Both rituals have significance beyond individual purpose in that they represent a commitment to traditional collective values. As Peltier asserts, "I am a Sun Dancer [...] If I am to suffer as a symbol of my people, then I suffer proudly" (14). In this way he looks upon his prison sentence as representative of his people's suffering. The conversion experience behind *Prison Writings* is both individually centred and collectively inspired, an escape from the punishing conditions of the prison as well as a statement of cultural commitment.

Peltier supplants Christian allegory with a restored valuation of indigenous spiritual practices. Yet he resists offering this sacred knowledge for his readers' consumption. Just he is about to disclose his experience in the sweat lodge, he withdraws with the admonition: "I have to stop here. Beyond this point it becomes utterly private, incommunicable. To put it into words would destroy it" (186). Peltier holds back from fully divulging the sacred revelations of the *inipi*. When he is about to bring the reader into the sweat lodge once again, he exercises the same restraint: "By now the door's closed and ... But, no, that's as far as I can take you here. The rest [...] cannot be told" (196). The refusal to tell all is an expression of reverence for the ritual, but it could also be read as a reminder to non-Aboriginal readers not to close the gap between Peltier's world and his/her own. Peltier's distance recalls the final words of Quiché-Guatemalan Rigoberta Menchú's *testimonio*: "I'm still keeping secret what I think no-one should know. Not even anthropologists or intellectuals, no matter how many books they have, can find out all our secrets" (247). Menchú's repeated reference to such "secrets" calls attention to the selectiveness of her account.[4] Her qualification reflects an awareness of the vulnerability that can result when cultural knowledge is ceded to outsiders. Similarly, what is sacred to Peltier and his culture has been withheld from his readers.

Peltier's refusal to submit everything to the public gaze can be viewed as a refusal of objectification and a roadblock in the way of the reader's passive edification. The response this text asks of its reader is ultimately one of action. Following Peltier's text is a postscript by editor Harvey Arden that channels the reader's attention to a prison lockdown that has blocked all communication with the author in the final stages of this text's publication. These developments return us to Peltier's immediate situation and disturb the stable reading experience that has, up until now, characterized the reader's involvement with this work. The suspended contact between Peltier and his editor—and by extension, Peltier and his reader—reminds us of the tenuous nature of the dialogue between the prison writer and his audience. Arden uses these developments to call for action, providing contact numbers to petition against Peltier's imprisonment and reminding the uninvolved reader of his/her implication in "the insidious injustice that has put him where he is" (220).

This text thus urges the non-indigenous reader to recognize his/her stake in Peltier's present situation. At times, this reminder of the reader's involvement borders on pointing out his/her complicity in this injustice. For instance, Peltier's following pronouncements on the U.S. government's disregard for indigenous people explicitly addresses a White readership:

> We are the people from whom you took this land by force and blood and lies. We are the people to whom you promised to pay, in recompense for all this vast continent you stole, some small pitiful pittance to assure at least our bare survival. And we are the people from whom you now snatch away even that pittance, abandoning us and your own honor without a qualm, even launching military attacks on our women and children and Elders, and targeting—illegally even by your own self-serving laws—those of us, our remaining warriors, who would stand up and try to defend them. (55)

The public's complicity in these violations becomes more explicit when Peltier asks, "America, when will you live up to your own principles?" (55). This edgier and more polemical tone is unlike the voice we encounter in the rest of *Prison Writings*. Much of Peltier's text takes the form of an appeal that seeks the reader's understanding. *Prison Writings* holds the two in balance, inviting the non-Native audience's identification while also moving this readership to understand its implication in the power relationship that keeps Peltier where he is. As Peltier discusses his submission for clemency with President Clinton's departure from office, he places the reader in this act of judgment: "I await their—and *your*—consideration and compassion" (172; emphasis Peltier's). This text aims at moving its audience and at convincing the reader of both Peltier's innocence and the legitimacy of his people's resistance.

Peltier makes a plea to a non-Native reader as well, seeking the reader's understanding of the conditions that preceded his imprisonment and the equally unjust conditions that continue in the prison. There is an invited identification as Peltier appeals to the reader's humanity and entreats him/her to recognize his imprisonment as yet another instance of the erosion of his people's dignity. He widens the possibilities of his readership as he wonders about the reader's identity and conditions of reading: "I try to imagine who you might be and where you might be reading this. Are you comfortable? Do you feel secure?" (7). In a gesture of apparent openness and sincerity, he invites the reader into his world: "Let me write these words to you, then, personally. I greet you, my friend. Thanks for your time and attention, even your curiosity" (7). This open baring of himself sets into motion his later identification with the reader. "*I am everyone*," he writes later in his text, "*Even you*" (39). With this rhetorical manoeuvre, he extends this identification in both directions to make the following argument: "When you exclude us, you exclude your own conscience" (47). This gesture outward can be read as a statement about the prisoner's significance to a non-imprisoned public readership. By constructing a collective body that includes the reader, Peltier urges his/her recognition of the larger social consequences of his imprisonment. Peltier, it should be noted, has amassed a large collective of supporters, including Nobel laureate Archbishop Desmond Tutu, numerous churches, and entertainment icons such as Robert Redford. The force of this cultural response cannot help but pull the reader into an illustrious and stalwart community of supporters.

In writing against the master discourses of law and Christianity, Peltier also performs a type of literary innovation on the level of genre. He describes the materials out of which he forms this text as "fragmentary sketches for an autobiography" (xxv), but he undercuts this expectation with this insertion: "I hope someday to write—which I'd originally thought would be enough" (xxv). With these words he frustrates any attempt to fix his writing and thereby limit it to a certain genre. As in *Stolen Life*, the bridging of different literary forms in *Prison Writings* suggests an experience or experiences that may lie outside the representational capabilities of a single genre. The text combines autobiography, political testimony, and poetry in a way that produces different registers of reading, registers that include the individual, historical, political, and legal. Peltier's text, like that of Wiebe and Johnson, seeks to adjust the legal and historical record. *Prison Writings* further shares with *Stolen Life* and *Inside Out* a grid-like movement between the individual and collective significance of the author's story.

Peltier uses his prison autobiography to refashion a collective identity for himself and to explore the relation between his present imprisonment and a broader cultural history. Despite a different intention expressed at the beginning of the work, however, he cannot cease to address the system that has incriminated him. The inability to disengage himself from the legal and judicial institutions that have taken away, in the absolute sense, his right to self-determination prompts a question that arises in relation to the rest of the prison texts examined in this half of the book: How is one to represent oneself independently in instances where the law has left its indelible mark?

Notes

1 Letter from Paul Berg addressed to the President of the United States. December 20, 2000. www.hartford-hwp.com/archives/41/367.html.

2 For further discussion on Aboriginal philosophies of healing and justice, and on some of the problems indigenous defendants encounter in Western courts, see Ross, *Returning to the Teachings*.

3 Dale Turner adds: "An Iroquoian concept of justice centres on the idea that all people can live in peaceful coexistence provided they respect the moral autonomy of the other" (53).

4 Menchú's "secrets" also shatter the illusion of immediacy—the expectation that this is an intimate, direct disclosure. The issue of immediacy has been at the centre of debate regarding this text. Some critics have unravelled Menchú's authority with attention to how the presence of anthropologist and collaborator Elisabeth Burgos-Debray frames the resulting text. More recent discussion about this work has called into question the "truthfulness" of Menchú's testimony. American anthropologist David Stoll discredited Menchú's account, claiming that it served primarily as propaganda for the Guerrilla Army of the Poor. Critics like Arturo Arias have countered Stoll's charges with further political contextualization. For a summary of the debate, see Arias.

TWO James Tyman's *Inside Out:* An Autobiography by a *Native Canadian*

Inside Out was written in six weeks while Tyman was serving a two-year prison sentence at Saskatoon Correctional Centre. Experimenting first with crime fiction, Tyman turned his attention to writing his life story—a story that, by the time he was twenty-four, included a lengthy rap sheet and a growing pattern of recidivism. Like Peltier, Tyman explores the devastating effects of racism and its relation to his present imprisonment. He does not experience the same poverty and material desperation as Leonard Peltier and Yvonne Johnson do. He is not spared, however, an insidious racism displayed by neighbours, classmates, and authority figures in his community. Tyman attributes his criminality to this racism—a causal relationship reflected in the three-part structure of his autobiography: Racism, Crime, Recovery. He had been adopted into a White, middle-class family, and many of the episodes in his early life describe his shame at his race as he struggled for acceptance in the community of his adopted family. Tyman repeatedly points out that it is not just his racial identity that is the root of his problems: he is without an individual identity. He has been denied the opportunity to acquire a sense of himself within his racial culture; at the same time, he is unable to feel entitled to the class privilege of his upbringing. This sense of identity he finds through crime.

Yet it is easy to situate Tyman's individual journey within the histories of Aboriginal people in Canada. His removal from his family, his attempt to acculturate out of his cultural heritage, and his struggle to regain a sense of indigenous identity are experiences not unfamiliar to many. The isolation Tyman experiences is in part a symptom of a larger history of colonization. In *A Recognition of Being: Reconstructing Native Womanhood*, Kim Anderson explains that this sense of disidentification is representative of many people of Tyman's generation: "Unfortunately, part of our experience as Native peoples includes being relocated, dispossessed of our ways of life, adopted into white families, and so on [...] For many of us, part of being Native is feeling like we aren't" (27). As Anderson describes, this cultural rupture manifests itself on an individual level. The result is a collective experience of alienation, a difficult alignment with one's cultural community. In a curious irony, then, this individual isolation is a collective condition.

Tyman's adoption could be seen as a continuation of the residential school legacy. In his study of Aboriginal child custody, Patrick Johnston observes that "as education ceased to function as the institutional agent of colonization, the child welfare system took its place" (24). In its most extreme form, this development became known as the "Sixties Scoop," when between 1955 and 1964, the number of Aboriginal children placed in the custody of provincial child welfare systems rose as much as 35 percent. Tyman was adopted at the tail end of this scoop, when the removal of Aboriginal children from their families had become a common occurrence. Although the Tymans offered a more nurturing environment than the residential school or, by comparison, other examples of foster care such as we encounter in Beatrice Culleton's novel *In Search of April Raintree* (1983), their withholding of vital information about his biological family and their failure to address his difference set him up for a difficult struggle. Consequently, he was denied easy cultural identification with both his adopted family *and* his biological one. He could not comfortably enjoy the class privilege of his adopted context; at the same time, he could not fully integrate with a Métis cultural community.

The first part of Tyman's autobiography explores his gradual, painful introduction to racism. Adopted at the age of four, he remembers very little of his early life except a single memory of abuse by his biological father. His individual encounters with racism feature most prominently in this first part of the narrative, but most poignant are the moments where he redirects this racism at other Aboriginal people. In the small Saskatchewan town of Fort Qu'Appelle, Aboriginal people reside on the fringes and are most often remarked on by the narrator in situations reflecting their disenfranchisement—"sleeping in the tall weeds behind the hotel on Main Street" or attracting notice for "their dirty clothes and hair" (11). Tyman's knowledge of indigenous people is formed through the stereo-types circulating within this dominant White community. His impressions of a nearby residential school, for instance, not far from the Catholic school he attends, are products of such fabulation:

> There was an Indian Residential School down the road in Lebret. It went around the schoolyard that if you were bad, the teachers would send you there. That terrified us because it was full of Indians. Conversations at recess molded my outlook toward them. Everything I heard was negative:
> "I hear they have to beat the Indians, to get them to learn."
> "My brother says Indians will steal your stuff." (12)

Jimmy early on notes the residential school's likeness to a prison: "The Residential School was more commonly referred to as a prison. When our bus drove by I found myself straining to see the gun towers, the barbed wire fence, the high cement wall" (12). His impression of this structure reveals a view of its occupants as dangerous miscreants. Jimmy acquires a fear of his own race, a fear that inevitably becomes directed inward:

> My parents treated me with love, but at school I learned of the Indians and their savage ways, how they scalped people, how they'd tie you across an anthill till the insects ate you alive. It chilled me to the bone to think of such a horrible death. I wondered if that was what the Indians did out on the reservations that surrounded Fort Qu'Appelle. We'd sit in class telling horror stories about how the Indians were going to come in and burn the village and scalp everybody. (15)

Jimmy sees Aboriginal people from his vantage point of middle-class insularity. His perception of his race is built on constructions whose veracity he lacks the discerning power to dismiss.

Jimmy's behaviour increasingly conforms to these racist constructions. In a particularly evocative moment in the text, he describes a Sunday school class led by his adopted mother. He marvels at the images of Jesus portrayed by the catechisms, the illustrations of angels playing harps, and notices another "fascinating thing [...] that there were no Indians floating around in the clouds" (13). "In fact," young Jimmy further notes, "there were no Indians at all in these books! Yes sirree, Indians were evil" (13). Immediately after this recognition, Tyman relates the following incident:

> Once I got hold of a Swiss Army Knife, and I was playing with it in Sunday School. When my mother asked what I was doing, I thrust it into the air. "Just playing with my knife, Mom." The other kids jumped.

My mother had a look of astonishment on her face. The next day I was questioned—in class, in the school ground, on the bus—about my brave, defiant act. I made new friends, and some kids stopped picking on me. I thought it was because they liked me. (13)

This passage marks a crucial moment in young Jimmy's identity. Unwittingly, he has reproduced the same behaviour as the racist constructions of Aboriginal people. His defiance attracts attention and fear, reactions that elevate him above his feelings of subordination.

When Tyman begins frequenting the bars of downtown Moose Jaw and other larger centres, he observes a "respect" given to the most feared criminals: "They were important. They were mostly of Indian ancestry and they were obviously criminals. But they had respect and fear, and apparently a lot of friends. I could sense it was wrong, but I wanted it. I wanted people to respect me in the same way. […] I wanted it, and I was going to get it" (66). Through his involvement in criminal activity, Tyman earns the respect he craves. As he becomes heavily entangled in pimping, drug dealing, and violent acts, and increasingly estranged from his family, his narrative takes on the qualities of a true crime novel. The violence Tyman exhibits, and his exploitation of women in particular, lead us to consider the potentially different ways that racism affects the authors in this study. Tyman re-enacts his denigration on the women around him. This internal pecking order we see in *Stolen Life*, especially in the abuse Johnson claims she suffered by her brother, Leon. Many of the crimes Tyman describes are senseless, without significant purpose or material cause. He struggles, as he does with the crimes of his youth, to explain or understand why he commits such acts.

Tyman finds a sense of belonging in the rugged subculture of skid row. This subculture becomes his community, a place of kinship in a modern sense—because of its urban, class basis—as well as a literal sense: it is here that he finds out about his genealogy and locates his biological mother. He describes the context of their meeting and the significance of finding his mother here:

It was a bar frequented by prostitutes, pimps, drug dealers and their customers, winos, ex-cons, perverts of every persuasion, people running from the law. My mother was not one of these. She drank there because it was where she was accepted for what she was—an Indian, like most of the other patrons. This was her place of refuge, her place to be with her own. (8)

Interestingly, Tyman mother's reasons for being there are similar to his own: for acceptance and belonging, free from racial or class prejudice. The people here are all outcasts and almost all Aboriginal.

Tyman is attracted to this setting from his first exposure to it, seduced by the alternative social recognition and status he can acquire here. He observes those who occupy this echelon of society: "They had identity. They were street people. That was their identity, their worth, and they loved it and accepted it. I wanted it" (70). The street is a place of belonging with its own values and hierarchy. For Tyman, it offers "entrepreneurial," self-making potential. In a discussion of her time spent on "the streets," Patricia Monture-Angus troubles any assumptions about the values and lessons one learns in this place. She cites, as an example, the frequent question of how she "made it" from the streets to the university. "The question presumes that there is intrinsically something 'better' about the university compared to the street. And the same goes for the people that occupy both spaces," she writes (47). "I have walked both roads," she reflects, "and I do not find that presumption to be true" (47). The significant difference, she maintains, "is that one type of knowledge is sanctioned and the other is disregarded" (47). For Tyman the subculture of the streets provides a group identity that he never fully acquires within the White, middle-class community of his adopted family.

Part of Tyman's sense of displacement is the result of his adopted family's minimizing of his racial and cultural background. While Jimmy would listen good-naturedly to the racist constructions of indigenous people circulating within his peer group, he admits he would later "go home and scrub [his] hands, hoping to wash the darkness off" (15). The "residue" of race keeps him from integrating invisibly into the cultural and social matrix of his adopted family. Like his inability to wash away the traces of his race, his adoption is similarly unable to wash away his racial and biological background. When Jimmy finds his adoption papers, he becomes a witness to his re-creation: "I came across a large brown envelope marked 'Saskatchewan Social Services Department.' My head went light [...] Then I finally found some news: 'Kenny Howard Martin was placed with William and Cecile Tyman on September 17th, 1967. His new name will be James Kenneth Tyman'" (25). This discovery puts his sense of identity into crisis. "Its impact on me was staggering," he summarizes (25). As Warren Cariou observes in "The Racialized Subject in James Tyman's *Inside Out*," the erasure of his family history is so complete that Tyman is surprised to discover he is Métis when he unearths his adoption papers. Seeing himself identified as "'the subject'" (25), he marvels at this new recognition of himself. "'I'm a subject,' I smiled to myself" (25). His adopted family, though supportive and loving, diminishes the significance of Jimmy's past, his parentage, and his birthplace. Later, when his mother asks him why he repeatedly commits criminal acts, "'Why? Didn't we give you everything?'" he silently responds: "I wanted to tell her that that wasn't the problem. I got everything I needed except a sense of identity" (64).

Because of his White, middle-class upbringing, Tyman feels alienated from his racial community. In the prison, however, he is able to enjoy an inverted racial hierarchy: "I was quickly accepted among the inmates. I was a solid guy, good people, a bro to my fellow Indians who made up 75% of the unit's population" (103). However, Tyman is also different from his counterparts. By Aboriginal people he is often identified as an "apple"—red on the outside, white on the inside. His adoption into a White family tends to soften the courts' view of him and results in shorter prison sentences. The contrast between him and another Aboriginal inmate emerges strikingly in the following exchange after Tyman wins an appeal:

> I walked onto the range shouting, "Justice has been done! We live in a free society where fairness and honesty are put on a pedestal! We the people should be ..."
> "Ah, shut the fuck up!" an Indian from Alberta spoke up.
> "Just because you're dogging it, doesn't mean I am," I said. "So go lock yourself in your drum and write poetry." (112)

Tyman is spared some of the reality experienced by other Aboriginal people because of his family's privilege. He is, for instance, spared the experience of attending the residential school—a structure that signifies young Jimmy's first exposure to the carceral containment of indigenous people. His middle-class upbringing shelters him from an understanding of the extent of poverty among Aboriginal people. Later, when he meets Donna, an Aboriginal woman who becomes his supportive and respected partner, he is shocked by the material deprivation she describes: "I learned of her upbringing, about life on the reserve near North Battleford. Poverty was the norm. There was no running water in most households. That shocked me. Didn't every household in Canada have running water?" (160). This self-dramatization, while perhaps seeming disingenuous, indicates Tyman's removal from the realities of other Aboriginal people. The economic stability of his domestic environment prevents him from knowing the full extent of what it is like to be an indigenous person in Canada. Though not without its own set of conflicts, his upbringing was far more materially secure than those of the Aboriginal people he encounters.

Tyman's transformation comes about as he manages to shed his shame at his race and view himself within a cultural collective. His political consciousness is precipitated by his discussions with another prisoner, Herbie, who lays bare the racism that resides within him: "After talking to Herbie about Indian people and their beliefs, I found that I was myself a hardcore racist. I felt disgusted with myself, remembering all the snide remarks I had made over the years about Indian people. They weren't a bunch of bloodthirsty savages. They were my own people" (109). Tyman's time in the prison generally, and his encounter with Herbie particularly, engenders a political awareness. An emerging sense of pride in his Nativeness marks a final stage in his development that constitutes the third and final part of the narrative, titled "Recovery." He returns to prison, this time for a crime he did not commit, with a changed awareness of himself: "The jail is the same [...] I have a new attitude this time, though. The hatred is gone. The shame of being Indian is not there" (226). This newly acquired confidence in his racial identity carries over into the publisher's "About the Author and Book" section, where Tyman declares: "'*Inside Out* was not written to seek pity nor was it done to ask forgiveness. I wrote this book to simply ask for understanding and acceptance for myself and all Native people'" (227). This statement calls to mind Peltier's self-positioning and claim of representativeness in his text.

While Tyman appears to turn away from a confessional mode in claiming to seek neither pity nor forgiveness, his plea for "understanding and acceptance" could also be read as a function of confession. Confession, Rita Felski points out, can go beyond the strict understanding of a plea for forgiveness to involve, rather, an intimate disclosure of self for the ultimate purpose of social reintegration or "acceptance." Stephen Spender further describes the confession's operation: "All confessions are from subject to object [...] Indeed, the essence of the confession is that the one who feels outcast pleads with humanity to relate his isolation to its wholeness" (120). Tyman's appeal outward—his seeking of readers' "understanding and acceptance"—is consistent with Spender's and Felski's formulations of confession. The intimate baring of self that we encounter in *Inside Out* is intended to elicit the reader's understanding and acceptance.

Tyman's avowal of recovery in the final pages contributes to this autobiography's confessional tenor. The fashioning of a redemptive narrative out of Tyman's story is most explicit in the publisher's postscript. Here, Tyman is described as having "taken on the job of rebuilding his life against incredible odds" by bettering himself educationally and economically (227). "All of us at Fifth House Publishers are privileged to have had the opportunity to work and be friends with this very courageous young man," the publishers' endorsement reads (227). The altruistic tone of this characterization is worth considering, because it raises the issue of readerly values—specifically, the desire for a story about the human ability to persevere through "incredible odds." These statements about the author are also interesting in that Tyman is reintegrated by an Aboriginal-run publishing house, a modern institution of his larger indigenous community. The problem with regard to Tyman's autobiography is that the affirmation of rehabilitation and recovery is neither explicitly developed nor therefore entirely credible within the narrative as a whole. The final section depicting the upswing in Tyman's life constitutes a comparatively small portion of the text. These changes come about after he exhibits callous and violent behaviour, transgressing even his own code of integrity by stabbing his partner, Donna, after she refuses to turn a trick for his financial gain. Tyman's professed change of lifestyle and attitude does not, as a narrative closure, bear the weight of the extreme aggression and self-hatred developed extensively in the pages preceding it. The narrative closure of this text is extraliterary in a sense: it consists of the "plot" that involves him with Fifth House and his revisiting of his "past self" through a therapeutic and rehabilitative lens. After the book's publication, Tyman was in and out of prison in Kingston. He died a few years later on the street.

Tyman's autobiography blends together confessional writing with a true-crime story. Bruce Franklin identifies two types of confession operating in prison writing up until the nineteenth century. These two traditions were precursors to the true-crime story. The first promoted a type of moral inculcation in which "the criminal narrator characteristically is confessing his or her own crimes and this confession, especially its moral lesson, is ostensibly for the purpose of the whole narrative" (126). The second type was more explicitly for entertainment, where the narrator's "life of rascality" (137) and adventurous episodes represented a world largely unknown to the reader. Franklin further observes that these two types of confession often occurred simultaneously. Even when moral instruction undergirded the telling, "the main interest [lay] in the vicarious participation in their thrilling, sordid adventures" (126). Franklin's discussion of these two registers speaks to the reader's experience in *Inside Out*. The reader's interest in this text may similarly balance vicarious experience and moral affirmation. The coalescence of two confessional traditions returns us to the earlier point that confession may not strictly involve an avowal of guilt for forgiveness, and that other values, on the part of both the reader and the writer, may come into play in the operation of the confessional text.

The title of Tyman's work, *Inside Out*, is a self-reflexive description of the type of work this autobiography performs in its seeking of "understanding and acceptance." The confession, as Spender describes above, signifies a movement outward from isolation to wholeness in its appeal to a community of readers. The title also speaks to a type of movement that almost all prison writing enacts. A number of prison publications bear a similar name; P4W's *Inside Looking Out*, Stony Mountain Penitentiary's *Inside-Outside*,[1] and the American journal of prison writing, *Inside/Out*, are just a few examples.[2] What issues and concerns accompany this movement to a non-imprisoned public? The politics of readership will continue to be a consideration in the rest of the prison texts discussed in this book. My examination will emphasize this literature's social function while also looking at the variety of genres the authors take up to speak beyond the barriers—physical, social, racial, intellectual—that consign them to the periphery of our imagination.

Notes

1 See Gaucher, "The Canadian Penal Press," for summaries of these publications' frequency and duration of circulation.
2 This journal publishes writing exclusively by incarcerated writers. See Bruchac, "The Decline and Fall of Prison Literature"; and the annotated bibliography in Harris and Aguero.

THREE Auto/biographical Jurisdictions

Collaboration, Self-Representation,
and the Law in *Stolen Life:
The Journey of a Cree Woman*

Yvonne Johnson is a woman of Cree and mixed blood serving twenty-five years to life in a Canadian prison. Convicted of first-degree murder in 1991 for the death of a Wetaskiwin man, she has served time at the Kingston Prison for Women (P4W), the Okimaw Ohci Healing Lodge in Saskatchewan, and, more recently, the Edmonton Institute for Women. She was an inmate at P4W when she contacted Rudy Wiebe in 1992. Moved by his novel *The Temptations of Big Bear* (1973)—his historiographic work about the Plains Cree leader who Johnson claims is her great-great-grandfather—she wrote a letter to the him revealing her genealogy and asking him to share the knowledge he had gained from his vigorous research. Wiebe admitted his mutual interest in "this self-aware, storytelling descendant of the historical Big Bear" (Wiebe and Johnson 14), and subsequently agreed to help Johnson write her story, undertaking a five-year collaboration that culminated in the publication of *Stolen Life*.

Johnson's imprisonment prompted her appeal to Wiebe to help her write her life story. The process of writing it reflected the way in which the law continues to restrict her agency. As a convicted prisoner, Johnson writes from a position of assumed culpability; as an author of this text, she does not start off on neutral footing with the reader. Her enlisting of Wiebe's editorial assistance suggests the challenges for self-representation that exist for an author who has been publicly condemned. Johnson was already writing before she met Wiebe, compiling the materials of her "life-story book" (40). Wiebe's presence in *Stolen Life* is not only as an editor and author, but also as Johnson's "representative." He moves from collaborator to advocate in the text, framing her account in a way that prepares the reader for a certain telling and, at times, doing the telling himself. In addition to examining the legalistic framework surrounding Johnson's testimony, then, I will also examine the effects of joint authorship on her self-representation. What narrative strategies does Wiebe deploy to generate confidence in Johnson's testimony? How is the reader called upon to adjudicate? As I examine the various discursive contexts in which Johnson testifies in *Stolen Life*, I will draw on a number of relevant concepts—collaboration, limit-cases, trauma, and witnessing—to explore their effect on the process of representation.

Yvonne Johnson did not testify at her trial for the murder of Leonard Charles Skwarok. Where her account might have intervened in the court's presentation of her, there is a silence, a crucial void in the testimonies and proceedings that indict her for first-degree murder.[1] Johnson's absent testimony is significant for a number of reasons. Most obvious, perhaps, is that she left herself to be represented by others—by her lawyer, by the prosecutor, and by other witnesses whose criminal sentences were reduced by their implication of her. Johnson maintains that she was represented before a word was spoken. Before an all-White, predominantly male jury, her presence, she interprets, was reduced to "an Indian face to judge and sneer at" (318). But Johnson's forfeited testimony can also be seen as a refusal to give voice in this specific context. Her silence retains the possibility of setting aright the public record, of testifying in a different medium. *Stolen Life* enters where this silence leaves off, filling in for the testimony not given in the courtroom.

Testimony is a term that has appeared with increasing frequency in recent literary discussions. What are the generic and discursive contours of testimony, and why, as Shoshana Felman asks, has it become "at once so central and so omnipresent in our recent cultural accounts of ourselves?" ("Education and Crisis" 6). Definitions of testimony centre on a constative process of verifying a statement or fact with written or spoken evidence. Among the more or less uniform definitions that appear in the *Oxford English Dictionary*, two usages are particularly evocative in understanding *Stolen Life*'s function as testimony. The first is an "open attestation or acknowledgment; confession, profession." Implicit in this definition is the submission to an external authority, possibly an admission of culpability. Johnson's confession to her involvement in the murder closely adheres to this understanding of testimony. Immediately following this definition is, however, another variation: "An expression or declaration of disapproval or condemnation of error; a protestation."[2] Testimony here signifies a petitioning against a situation or statement, an apology similar to Peltier's use of testimony in *Prison Writings*. Accordingly, *Stolen Life* provides a separate hearing for Johnson to respond to her representation in the court and for Wiebe to denounce the legal manoeuvrings that made her primarily culpable for the crime. It is between these two functions of testimony—an act of confession and an act of protestation—that Johnson's testimony operates.

Away from its broader dictionary understanding, testimony has acquired specific meaning in a number of critical contexts. Its currency in Holocaust accounts, Latin American documentary literature, illness narratives, and social justice commissions indicates the transvaluation of this term from its strictly legalistic sense. "Witnessing" and "testimony" are words that have also been applied to contemporary accounts by indigenous writers in Canada and the United States.[3] These accounts testify to past traumas that, in Dominick LaCapra's words, "are just coming to a fully articulate voice in the present" (171). LaCapra suggests that the relatively recent emergence of these accounts is not singularly a result of the delayed effects of trauma, but also the result of a mass culture's reluctance to look at a contemporary trauma in which it is implicated. Other critics have made the comparison between Holocaust testimonies and an emergent body of indigenous writing.[4]

In their work on trauma and witnessing, Shoshana Felman and Dori Laub identify the psychoanalytic, literary, and historical dimensions of testimony that make it a germane mode for bearing witness to trauma. Paralleling the process of witnessing that Felman and Laub theorize, Johnson reconstructs traumatic episodes of her past and transmits them to Wiebe, who serves as a secondary witness to the trauma. The merging of therapeutic and historical discourses that Felman and Laub identify as a key function of testimony corresponds to the different registers on which Johnson's traumatic past is read in *Stolen Life*. Johnson's individual experiences of trauma hold historical import by evoking a larger, collective experience of colonization. Testimony, as it is revalued in *Stolen Life*, transcends its legalistic definition to bear witness to the injustices Johnson has suffered.

The collective significance of Johnson's life narrative calls to mind another instance of testimony that has emerged out of political resistance movements of colonized peoples. Testimony, or *testimonio*, refers to a literary form from Latin America. These accounts address a situation of racial, cultural, or class struggle in which the narrator is actively and presently a part. The *testimonio* involves a model of production similar to the one that Felman and Laub discuss as testimony. A crucial difference between the two is that while the latter bears witness to an event of the historic past, the *testimonio* typically engages a present, insurgent situation. *Stolen Life* is an interesting convergence of these two conceptions of testimony.

In the two instances of testimony described above, an interlocutive process between narrator and interviewer brings forth the resultant text. Johnson and Wiebe's text follows a similar model of exchange in its production and so prompts a set of considerations pertinent to collaborative life writing, ethnography, and oral history. Collaborative life narratives cross a range of disciplines in the subjects they involve and in the histories they document. Whether as "autobiography by those who do not write," as Philippe Lejeune calls it, or as "salvage ethnography," which is James Clifford's term, collaborative life writing brings with it a rather troubled history because of the unequal power relationship traditionally at play in the production of the text. Such a text typically involves a transaction between a narrating subject who does not have access to literary or publishing institutions and an editor who is representative of a more powerful social class. Recent collaborative life writing shows an acuity toward this inequity and has developed an increasingly self-critical element. In *Stolen Life*, Wiebe demonstrates a similar sensitivity toward the different positions he and Johnson occupy in relation to each other. In a conversation with Johnson's counsellor, Wiebe expresses his reluctance toward this undertaking: "'I'm an aging, professional man, exactly the kind of 'powerful White' who's so often created problems for her. Isn't there someone else who should work with her, a woman, a Native writer?'" (41). Wiebe's uncertainty here reflects an awareness of the different, charged histories he and Johnson bring to this text—histories that will have an inevitable impact on the production and reception of this work.

Furthermore, Wiebe's self-consciousness needs to be contexualized within the voice appropriation debate in Canada. Emerging in the late 1980s and early 1990s, this debate had a lasting impact on the reception and activity of non-indigenous authors writing about Aboriginal cultures. Encapsulated in the title of Lenore Keeshig-Tobias's 1988 article, "Stop Stealing Native Stories," this sensibility identified an urgent need for indigenous authors, artists, and critics to be the crafters of their own representations. A number of Aboriginal-led creative organizations have emerged in response—among these, the Committee to Re-establish the Trickster,[5] the En'owkin International School of Writing,[6] and presses such as Theytus Books. Although many eminent indigenous critics, including Keeshig-Tobias and Maria Campbell, have noted his sensitive handling of Aboriginal subjects and history, Keeshig-Tobias deems Wiebe incapable of "assuming a Native voice" (Lutz 80). She gravely adds: "The people who have control of your stories, control of your voice, also have control of your destiny, your culture" (81).

Stolen Life is a mediated text, which is not to say that it is unethical or politically condemnable, but that it needs to be read with this sense of mediation at the front of the reader's mind. Wiebe is the relay—literally and literarily—between Johnson and the reader. We can never forget this and the effects it has on the narrative. In his discussion of the ethics of collaborative life writing, G. Thomas Couser points out: "The inherent imbalance between the partners' contributions may be complicated by a *political* imbalance between them; often, collaborations involve partners whose relation is hierarchized by some difference—in race, culture, gender, class, age, or (in the case of narrators of illness or disability) somatic condition" (336). To Couser's listing I would add the physical and ideological limitations the prison places on the incarcerated writer. Wiebe is Johnson's link— at times her only link—to the outside. What is more, he represents a link to Johnson's ancestral history, an ancestry that, she claims, includes legendary Plains Cree leader Mistahimaskwa (Big Bear). It is Johnson who initiates their correspondence in an unsolicited letter to Wiebe. In it, she describes her esteem for *The Temptations of Big Bear*: "*I was slapped in the face by how much you really knew or could understand*" (8). She entreats him, "*Please help me share what it is you know, and how you got it*" (9). "*In my own research I find everyone shutting up on me [...]. I run into special difficulties because of where I am*" (8). Wiebe's value to Johnson is not initially as someone who can help her write her life story, but as someone who can supply her with his own extensive and impressive body of research about her larger body of kin "*that has been sent all over the four winds*" (9; all italics in original).

Ethical issues inevitably surround any collaborative textual production, especially those that set out to record the life of one of its subjects. Focusing attention on these problems should not, however, detract from a recognition of the ways in which a co-author's presence is enabling to the primary subject's articulation. One might ask, for instance, whether a text like *Stolen Life* would have been brought to publication without Wiebe's assistance. (The counter-argument here is exactly this: not a text of this sort, but possibly a different one.) However, Wiebe's editorial and authorial presence has critical effects both on Johnson's self-representation and on the value attributed to her life narrative. What thematic effect does Wiebe's ordering of the narrative achieve, and how does Johnson's imprisonment fit into this overall thematic structure?

The initial problems of the collaboration were more practical. Johnson's counsellor pointed out to Wiebe: "'She's not capable of writing a publishable book, and never in P4W'" (40). It was not only psychic stress that Johnson had to work through, but also material, physical constraints that hindered her ability to write. Remembering his first visit to Johnson at P4W, Wiebe remarks how this obtrusive structure blots out the lives of those who enter "this stone place designed for lifetimes of confinement, where blurred shouts boom and echo along grey corridors and barred steel seems to be slamming continuously" (22). "The entire building seems to heave [...] breathing hard and blowing away the spirits of all the women it has sucked up," Wiebe says when he paraphrases Johnson on this topic (22). He recalls their first meeting in this place: "When the barred door slid aside on the dark, sounding corridors and stairs of P4W and I saw her for the first time, it seemed that, despite our long telephone conversations, she was materializing out of prison blankness, that she was coming towards me contained in a kind of silence that would surely be indecipherable to me" (21). What Johnson, in part, writes against is the silence that this place attempts to impose on her. The challenge for both authors will be to translate what is "indecipherable." "Neither of us yet has a true conception of how difficult it will be to tell her story," Wiebe later reflects. "After forty years of working at writing, I think I know a bit about making stories, but I don't grasp the impossibilities of this one; not yet" (24).

Stolen Life is an instance of what Leigh Gilmore calls a "limit-case"— writing that "breaks the frame" to "establish a lyrical position for the subject of trauma as one that entangles violence, memory, kinship, and law" (8). Limit-cases, Gilmore points out, often have no precedent. "'In certain ways she doesn't grasp the magnitude of her own story,'" Johnson's counsellor tells Wiebe (41). Wiebe expresses his initial wonder at the type of writing this book will become. "I know about writing certain kinds of books," he thinks to himself, "but I know I know nothing about the one this will have to be" (41). His response speaks to the difficulty not only of writing a text with a subject who is in prison, but also of finding a suitable narrative form for a story that has so many different values relevant to it. It is Johnson's traumatic past, however, that will pose the most significant challenge for this collaboration. What mode of writing can represent the memories that Johnson is about to disinter? As Johnson begins producing pages upon pages of "separate, lone memories, individual acts, but seemingly connected," she asks herself, "Do I really want to know and what am I to do with them?" (41).

The different genres and narrative modes summoned in Stolen Life reflect the difficulty of writing a life that has so many levels of signification—a life that bears the weight of the post-contact history of Aboriginal people, of personal trauma inflicted by her own family members, and a life sentenced behind bars for murder. Thematically, these different levels fit together with historical causality. To his own series of questions about Johnson's life lived *in extremis*—"Why has she lived such a dreadful life, and why has she been so destructive to herself and those she loves? Why have they been so devastatingly destructive to her? How is it she became entangled in murder?"—Wiebe answers, "What I already know of her life makes it almost too horrifically representative of what has happened to the Native people of North America; of what her ancestor Big Bear most feared about the ruinous White invasion that in his time overwhelmed him, that jailed him in Stony Mountain Prison in 1885 for treason-felony, that is, for 'intending to levy war against the Queen, Her crown and dignity'" (16).Johnson's life story takes its place within a succession of cultural disinheritance and an ancestral legacy of criminalization. Four generations later, Big Bear's grim prophecy of the fate of his inheritors is confirmed. At the 1876 signing of Treaty Six, which Big Bear refused to sign at the time, he reportedly uttered: "'There is one thing that I dread: to feel the rope around my neck'" (Wiebe and Johnson 10). Cast within this continuum, Johnson's situation is easy enough to understand. The victim of extreme and, for many readers, unimaginable abuse, poverty, and racially motivated violence, Johnson struggled even for her daily survival. She later writes, "'I see now that most children, growing up, are taught options, choices, personal strategies. I never was, and even though I understood that choices must exist, they couldn't mean anything to a dirty 'breed' like me. There were just two possibilities: get by, or commit suicide'" (141).

"Get by" and "hang on" are the lessons Johnson learns growing up. The first half of *Stolen Life* traces in often horrific detail Johnson's early brutalized life. Along with growing up a "halfbreed" in Butte, Montana—a mining city that lives by "eating its own guts" (80)—she was born with a double-cleft palate that limited her speech and resulted in years of painful operations. She suffered sexual and physical abuse within the home and lost her eldest brother in a death suspected to have been committed by the police. The first half of the text consists of Wiebe's reproduced dialogues between himself and Johnson; Johnson's journal entries, which document her process of remembering traumatic fragments of her past; and Wiebe's narrativized re-creation of episodes of Johnson's life. This structuring is significant because it steers our perception of Johnson's life and her later participation in the murder. The relationship between Wiebe and Johnson and the process of witnessing they undertake frame the telling for the first half of *Stolen Life*. Trauma expert Dori Laub describes this process and the role of the listener/witness within it: "To a certain extent, the interviewer-listener takes on the responsibility for bearing witness that previously the narrator felt [s]he bore alone, and therefore could not carry out. It is the encounter and the coming together between the survivor and the listener, which makes possible something like a repossession of the act of witnessing. This joint responsibility is the source of the reemerging truth" ("An Event Without a Witness" 85).

Laub emphasizes the trust and reciprocity integral to the witnessing act. For much of the text the reader serves as proxy witness to Johnson's trauma. By "proxy witness," I mean the reader's mediation in the process of witnessing—a role also addressed by Felman, who points out that the act of reading can be an act of bearing witness. In *Stolen Life* the reader's role is similar to Wiebe's, except, of course, with a crucial difference: Johnson's account has already been filtered by Wiebe. In this regard, her story loses the immediacy of survivor testimony as it is reworked into coherent, chronological, and stylistically refined prose.

Stolen Life is structured in such a way that the reader hears of Johnson's personal history and repeated victimization before s/he comes to know about her involvement in the murder. Johnson's indictment for first degree murder exists only in the background until midway in the text with the "Three Days in September" chapter. Wiebe assumes the central narrative voice in this and the following two chapters discussing Johnson's case. He moves, then, from witness to her trauma to advocate in a legal sense. He attempts to piece together a coherent picture of the events from a mass of information. "From police and witness statements, trial records, and Yvonne's recollections," he self-reflexively explains, "I have tried to clarify a logical strand of facts" (252). Wiebe creates a narrative context modelled after judicial process—a process that allows "for the dialogue of oppositions to expose the factual truth" (314). Shoshana Felman describes the function of testimony within this judicial process: "Testimony is provided, and is called for, when the facts upon which justice must pronounce its verdict are not clear, when historical accuracy is in doubt and when the truth and its supporting elements of evidence are called into question. The legal model of the trial dramatizes, in this way, a contained, and culturally channeled *crisis of truth*" ("Education and Crisis" 6; emphasis in original). The very basis of this process, Felman points out, is a "crisis of truth." In *Stolen Life*'s treatment of the trial, Johnson's missing testimony produces this crisis; its absence casts doubt on the entirety and conclusiveness of the court's assemblage of information. "What the testimony does not offer," Felman continues, is "a completed statement, a totalizable account of those events. In the testimony, language is in process and in trial, it does not possess itself as conclusion, as a constatation of a verdict or the self-transparency of knowledge" (5). Testimony, as Felman describes it, is only ever partial. In a way that demonstrates this fissuring of truth, Wiebe brings in legal statements and transcriptions of court proceedings, which he counterpoints with Johnson's personal account. But by this point in the text, Johnson has won the reader's confidence in the sincerity of her narration. While the reader's role is to adjudicate among the competing versions of truth brought out before him or her, the reading jury is tipped in Johnson's favour. The crisscrossing of perspectives, then, serves plausibly, if not conclusively, to undo the authority of the court proceedings that led to Johnson's conviction.

Wiebe's roles as narrator and advocate become conflated in the chapters that sort through the details of the murder. He reproduces witness statements and legal testimonies but mediates between these various accounts to reserve the ultimate authority in his reconstruction of the events: "I have studied [Johnson's version of events], at length, and researched more—including, of course, the trial records—and to create a reasonable account of this day I can only draw out the absolutely necessary strands of details, sketch what seem to be the most crucial and inevitable scenes. What is clear to us both is that, until the very last minutes before midnight, nothing criminal at all need ever have happened" (239–40).

Wiebe's reconstruction of the events is not only "logical," it is "reasonable," "necessary," "crucial," and "inevitable." As narrator, he attributes motivations and emotions to the characters he represents. In his re-creation of a "cell shot," in which undercover RCMP Constable Bradley sits with the co-accused Dwayne Wenger and Ernie Jensen, Wiebe interpolates: "In a minute Constable Jones will give Bradley the prearranged signal that will get him out of here, but even as he thinks this, he studies the two doomed men once more, carefully, with a trained eye and memory of a professional witness who knows he will be cross-examined by lawyers in a court of law. Poor buggers" (297). An omniscient narrator, Wiebe fills in the skeleton of facts, colours the events with emotional responses, even re-creates a voice for some of the characters involved. His reconstruction of the events successfully conveys an impression of Johnson as someone who found herself involved in a crime not by premeditation, but by the proliferation of suspicion that the victim of the murder was molesting Johnson's daughter. He describes the escalating tension on the night of the murder when Chuck Skwarok was invited to Johnson's apartment. According to Johnson, her cousin, Shirley Anne Salmon, had been floating suspicions that Skwarok sexually abused Johnson's daughter. In Wiebe and Johnson's characterization, Salmon emerges as the one who orchestrated the confrontation and manipulated Johnson into believing Skwarok guilty of such acts. A confrontation with Skwarok ensued on his arrival, which escalated into a violent attack by Johnson, Salmon, and two others present that night, Ernest Jensen, and Johnson's partner, Dwayne Wenger.

Johnson admits her participation in the violent assault on Skwarok in her basement, but she maintains that the greater part of the violence was waged by Salmon and Jensen. Salmon received the lightest sentence—twenty months for aggravated assault—and while Salmon and Wenger were given individual trials, Johnson and Jensen were tried together. A key witness in Johnson and Jensen's trial, Salmon gave testimony that in Wiebe's estimation "laid the basis in the jury's mind for Yvonne's first-degree murder conviction" (407). Wiebe focuses attention on Salmon's often contradictory versions of the events of that night, adding, "Yvonne insists that, in testifying as she did, her cousin lied over and over again" (407). In the end, Johnson emerges as someone caught in a crime, set up for disaster by an untrustworthy relative and by the vicissitudes of a night gone awry by heavy drinking. He relates the drastic turn Johnson's life takes after the hellish scene that occurred under the influence of alcohol. In the aftermath of the murder, Johnson awakes to realize that "when the law-enforcement system seizes you as a criminal, the world changes. You may never recognize yourself again" (281). In the stroke of a sentence, the adversary becomes the law, and the victim, Johnson. The evidence brought out in *Stolen Life*, partially reconstructed, partially rendered into fiction by Wiebe's narrating, contributes to Johnson's exoneration.

Near the end of the text, Johnson gives a detailed account of the night of the murder. Her confession marks a pivotal moment for the narrative since it is not collaborative. Wiebe signals to the reader that it is Johnson's voice speaking here: "In the following excerpts, taken verbatim from the tapes, the events of that dreadful evening are seen through Yvonne's eyes" (396). Her confession appears with some elliptical omissions and is transcribed from the five recorded audiotapes she presents to Wiebe. In terms of narrative effect, Johnson's protracted confession serves a few functions: first, it clears a space for Johnson's emergence as a protagonist of the narrative in the majority of the text preceding it. Next, the delay re-enacts the process that Wiebe must respect as Johnson's witness. He tells us, "To write the whole story, I need to hear her memory of the basement, but I cannot push her. So, I wait" (308). The restraint exercised by Wiebe coincides with LaCapra's and Laub's dictum that the secondary witness must abstain from inducing a reliving of the trauma. It is five years into their collaboration before Johnson divulges the details of the murder. Before offering her version of the events, she emphasizes the spiritual importance of the telling and indicates the presence of another interlocutor for this process: "I have taken Pauline Shirt as my Elder, and she is present with me at the Okimaw Ohci Healing Lodge while I tell this, for spiritual support, guidance, counselling, and for friendship [...] I do this in a ceremonial way, and it is covered under the medicine, and I believe the spirits are here to help me. My sole purpose in doing this is to give to the Creator" (396).

Confession, as a convention of the prison autobiography, typically signifies "an attempt to rethink the author's 'crimes' in relation to his [or her] own cosmology" (Davies 106). This tradition Johnson situates within a specific spiritual context, her Cree cosmology. But as she asks the reader, "Please try to hear me with your spirit" (396), she makes an appeal to moral justice, a gesture of confidence in justice as an indwelling, universal value.

The spiritual significance Johnson attaches to her confession prompts consideration of the public and private function of testimony. When Johnson refers to her "conviction of guilt, both legal and personal" (330), she distinguishes between the separate jurisdictions of personal (spiritual) and legal judgment. But as Leigh Gilmore points out, the confession sets out a double demand for the testifying subject. "Any self-representational act," Gilmore observes, "is fully burdened by its public charge to disclose a private truth" (14). The confession, while an intimate, introspective act, inevitably directs itself outward. Gilmore explains: "The confession welds together an official and a spiritual discourse in a way that conflates a functional boundary between the public and the private. This boundary dissolves under scrutiny in the confession, for just as one is compelled to express one's private self, the official rules for doing so are always foregrounded" (14). Johnson calls attention to the demand that Gilmore similarly underscores. In a witness statement describing her brother's rape of her, she reveals, "I have a hard time writing officially, as you would wish" (336). With this statement, she appears to turn away from "official" testimony to favour the more intimate act of witnessing. As Laub describes, "The witnesses are talking to *somebody*: to somebody they have been waiting for for a long time" (70–71; emphasis Laub's). Johnson follows by saying, "For the first time, I get a sense someone hears me, or wants to ..." (336).

Witnessing, as a private discourse addressed to another, offers Johnson a sense of legitimacy denied within an official, legal context. When Johnson testifies formally before a court against her brother, her testimony is dismissed and the charges against him dropped. In both her murder trial and her charges against her brother for sexual assault, the court bases its ruling on "credibility." Wiebe points out the class and race biases behind this value in the following dialogue reproduced from his consultation with various attorneys:

> Question: [...] if a person—especially a poor person from a racial minority [...] goes to trial, one shouldn't really expect justice. One can only expect what the judge or jury, who are invariably of the majority race, will find "believable"?

Answer: I wouldn't say "only expect." One always hopes that what is believable and what is just to all concerned are the same thing. [One hopes.] (314; Wiebe's parenthetical insertion)

What is "believable," Wiebe points out, is neither a neutral nor an objective judgment. The inclusion of the court case in which Johnson testifies to her rape provides a way of reading Johnson's silence in the central court case of this text—the murder of which she is found guilty. Its role is to show that when she does speak within a court of law, her credibility is dismissed. What is more, it demonstrates that the law does not protect her as a victim.

While Johnson expresses difficulty with the official medium of legal testimony, she nevertheless comes forth with a very public text. When the court refuses to acknowledge the truths she forces into the open, she turns to writing to find this sense of acknowledgment. "This should not have to be spoken in public, or in a court of law," Johnson says of her charges against her brother. "At best it should have been talked through in my family only. If only that were possible" (333). Her writing intervenes in the silence both she and her family have maintained, a silence that has been crippling to Johnson's sense of herself as a subject. The importance of confronting what one has been reluctant to acknowledge is reinforced in the very first sentence of *Stolen Life*, where Wiebe writes, "To begin a story, someone in some way must break a particular silence" (3). In Dori Laub's words, "The 'not telling' of the story serves as a perpetuation of its tyranny" (79). In such instances, "the events become more and more distorted in their silent retention and pervasively invade and contaminate the survivor's daily life. The longer the story remains untold, the more distorted it becomes in the survivor's conception of it, so much so that the survivor doubts the reality of the actual events" ("An Event Without a Witness" 79). With her investment in writing as a form of testimony, Johnson is able to affirm the reality of her flashbacks, whose veracity she had begun to doubt. LaÇapra summarizes the special function of testimony in acknowledging what one has struggled to integrate cognitively. "Testimonies," he formulates, "are significant in the attempt to understand experience and its aftermath, including the role of memory and its lapses, in coming to terms with—or denying and repressing—the past" (86–87). In instances of trauma, memory is a crucial nexus of self and subjectivity formation.

At what point does witnessing turn from an intimate, private discourse into a public act? One of the epigraphs to *Stolen Life* is a line from Albert Camus's *Myth of Sisyphus:* "But crushing truths perish from being acknowledged" (n.p.). The invocation of Camus, the Algerian-born French writer who used his writing to bear witness to the traumas of the Second

World War, invites consideration of Johnson's work as a similar testimonial act, one that testifies to a trauma that remains unacknowledged—individually and publicly. Both a "medium of healing" and a "medium of
historical transmission" (Felman, "Education and Crisis" 9), testimony bears
witness to a personal and collective trauma. "Trauma is never exclusively
personal," notes Leigh Gilmore. "Remembering trauma entails contextual-
izing it within history" (31). This thinking is echoed by Cathy Caruth, who
puts it: "History, like trauma, is never simply one's own [...] history is pre-
cisely the way we are implicated in each other's traumas" (24).

Johnson's trauma is also the trauma of her cultural community. The
question that follows, then, is this: Is this strictly Johnson's story to tell?
To her insistence that she must tell her story to break the silence surrounding her abuse, Wiebe responds, "'Yes—but it'll be hard. There are so many
people in your life, no story is ever only yours alone'" (24). After some
thought, Johnson counters, "'Maybe not only my story—but it is mine.
Others maybe won't agree, but I want to tell my life the way I see it'" (24).
Both Wiebe and Johnson anticipate opposition to her story, specifically
from members of Johnson's family who resent the unflinching exposure of
their private lives or deny the validity of her account. Johnson under-
stands that by speaking she will be rejected, even condemned by those
close to her. But while her disclosure of painful memories is an act of individual healing, it is not for her sake alone. She tells Wiebe, "'I try to tell
my sisters I've made a way for them to follow, I can take it, I've laid myself
down like a bridge, all they have to do is walk over me'" (24). Many of her
family members, however, refuse the story she tells. In this way, Johnson's
desire for collective belonging is upset by her most immediate collective
group, her family.

Johnson's rejection by her family undermines her characterization as
"representative," as standing in for a plural, collective "we." While her
experiences speak to a larger, cultural struggle, a deeply personal, individual "I" emerges in many of the memories she recounts. Hers is a pathos
of acute isolation that stems from early childhood and from a difference
marked by the physical deformity of a cleft palate. She explains, "My basic
problem was the way I was born; in the centre of my face, where my nose,
top lip, gums, and roof of my mouth should have been, there was only
folded tissue that left a gap in my upper mouth. Even my teeth and inner-
mouth bones were affected by this severe deformity. I've now had endless reconstructive surgery, but I still wonder what I would look like if I'd
been born like my sisters, all so neatly beautiful, and my brothers, so hand-
some as well" (29).

Johnson explains that this defect led to difficulty speaking and began
a frustrating ordeal to communicate. Johnson returns to this image of

herself as a mute child, an image that connects with the unspeakableness of many of her experiences:

> It was like being deaf but still hearing, speaking but speechless—it was there, heaping up inside me. I could not ask questions, just puzzle everything around inside my head, dreaming it, bouncing it back and forth, without any guidance to help me understand. So I learned by instinct [...] To depend only on myself. There was no one else.
>
> My mind was my best, really my only, companion. But I think that then, on a deeper level, my spirit already knew and understood how much I was being hurt. The impact I wore in silence, and shed in tears. (30)

This is an early portrait of Johnson, whose alienation begins with an inability to express herself in the most fundamental of ways. Johnson internalizes her difference by removing herself from others. Her response, she points out, is to depend solely on herself. This self-dependency grows into apprehension, mistrust, even hostility, toward others. Coupled with the sexual and physical abuse she suffers at the hands of family members and strangers, Johnson's physical self-consciousness leads to social isolation. She tells Wiebe, "There are lots of reasons I don't want people close to me. My lip is only one" (31).

Alongside Wiebe's treatment of Johnson's life story as representative of an entire people and history, then, is a quietly divergent perspective told by Johnson, whose cleft palate—while perhaps a "manifest gift" of a potent ancestral legacy[7]—results in her isolation from others, and whose individual experiences of abuse (which Wiebe reads as a collective, colonial condition) are the source of a fierce mistrust. Johnson's conception of identity pulls between competing configurations, between a sense of place within her rather formidable ancestral history and a painful awareness of her individual alienation. When Wiebe likens Johnson's silence in the courtroom to that of her ancestor—"Like her ancestor Big Bear at his trial for treason-felony in 1885, she did not speak a word in her own defence" (318)—he looks past the individuality of the life experiences that have forced Johnson into this state of silence. This silence is a behaviour that she learned early in response to the intimation of guilt. She summarizes her childhood: "living was a long, silent secret where the very act of breathing already made me guilty of something" (78). Much of this guilt has to do with her gender, as the following prohibitions reveal: "never sit with your legs apart, never forget to wear long pants under your dress or they'll see your panties if you forget yourself and play as a child will play, never talk back, never, ever look them in the eye but listen to every sound, watch, be always alert and ready to outmanoeuvre danger before it's close enough to catch you" (78). Johnson learns at an early age how to recognize the approach of danger. When she is arrested by police, her exercise of self-preservation is this learned silence. "They are in control," Wiebe narrates. "Except for one thing: her silence. Question, questions, let them pull out strands of hair, even offer them more—here, take it [...] Long ago she knew this, as a tiny child she was taught this over and over: cry if you must, but don't speak a word. Not to anyone" (284). While silence, as the proverbial statement goes, is a right, it is just as likely to be an act of defencelessness. Moreover, it can be perceived as an admission of guilt, which is how the jury in Johnson's trial most likely read her silence in the courtroom.

A point to which I wish to return here is that the specificity of Johnson's trauma complicates the organizing principle of this text, in which Johnson's experiences, including her present imprisonment, come to be read as representative of an entire people. In "Telling Trauma: Generic Dissonance in the Production of *Stolen Life*," Susanna Egan similarly questions "the one single and forceful meaning" that this text emphasizes—"that Yvonne's long history of abuse, with its apparently natural result of crime and imprisonment, mirrors the history and present situation of her peoples" (22–23). The thematic coherence into which Johnson's life story is yoked Egan finds "too tidy for the mess of trauma" (23). Egan's attention to the limitations that trauma places on narrative reconciliation is consonant with what we know about trauma and its resistance to progressive structure and resolution. As LaCapra explains, "working through trauma involves the effort to articulate or rearticulate affect in a manner that may never transcend, but may to some viable extent counteract, a reenactment, or acting out, of that disabling dissociation" (42). The resolution achieved by the end of *Stolen Life* runs counter to the continual intrusion of traumatic memory in the life of the victim. It also fails to hold up in light of recent developments in Johnson's case. While unable to "free" Johnson physically, the narrative repeatedly returns to her residency at the Okimaw Ohci Healing Lodge as a thematic end to her journey. The impression that Johnson has arrived at a place of origins and healing at the Okimaw Ohci Healing Lodge is undercut, however, by the reality that a few years after this text's publication, Johnson was transferred involuntarily to the Edmonton Institute for Women.[8] A post-narrative development not unlike the lockdown at Leavenworth, this incident returns us to Johnson's reality in the prison. Clearly, one of the principal players this text underestimates is Correctional Services Canada, whose power extends beyond the jurisdictions of this narrative to suspend the inmate's agency and self-determination at any time. Johnson's present state of imprisonment, like her traumatic past, is a condition that is impossible to transcend.

Egan remains similarly unconvinced by this narrative resolution and by the historical continuum that attempts to hold together the different generic registers in *Stolen Life*. The different textual registers in *Stolen Life*—testimony, literature, and scriptotherapy[9]—Egan sees as rubbing against one another, creating "dissonance" and leaving many issues, including Johnson's authorial agency and this work's generic integrity, unsettled. While I agree with Egan's criticism of Wiebe's omniscience as narrator and of his fixation on creating "a hero to succeed Big Bear" (Egan 18), I also see the different genres that Wiebe employs and the problems that Egan cites as evidence of the very difficulty of telling a story like this. Repeatedly throughout the work, Wiebe refers to the challenging process of amassing this text—a self-reflexivity that in fact undercuts Egan's appraisal of Wiebe as detached from the narrative, as erasing from the narrative his filtering of it. Notwithstanding Egan's view that Wiebe "claims no personal need to tell this story [...] nor any personal involvement in it" (14), Wiebe demonstrates an often upfront sensitivity to his and Johnson's different subject positions. In contrast to Egan's argument of Wiebe's uninvolved, omnipotent stance, my own reading sees Wiebe's personal and professional stake in this story as ever present in this text—to the extent that his own motives and desires explicitly imprint themselves on Johnson's life story.

It is far easier to criticize a text like *Stolen Life* than it is to prescribe alternative ways of presenting Johnson's life narrative. Johnson, we must keep in mind, presided over the making of this text. To dismiss or overlook this point is, in some ways, to dismiss her authority. Couser points out that "The justice of the portrayal has to do with whether the text represents its subject the way the subject would like to be represented, with whether that portrayal is in the subject's best interests, with the extent to which the subject has determined it" (338). Interestingly, though, these methods of calibrating the ethical performance of collaborative texts belie the equity that Couser defends. Such criteria fail to take into account ethical considerations that are not reducible to the individual or the individual life story. Authorship and appropriation remain sites of ongoing struggle in certain cultural contexts. In such cases, consideration must reach beyond universal, humanist judgments—with their assumption of individual agency—to acknowledge the different values that authority, self-representation, and agency may carry. It is these very issues that have been at the centre of debate over Aboriginal literary self-representation.

Rather than seeing the different genres and narrative modes in *Stolen Life* as masking problems with authorship and story making, however, one could view them as actively drawing attention to problems with voice, authority, credibility, and truth. *Stolen Life* is an instance of the innovation and intervention that are currently overhauling traditional applications of auto/biography. Such a text, as Gilmore notes of limit-case narratives, points to the "new ways of representing the individual in relation to personal and collective histories of abuse that are becoming possible [...] the new sorts of subjectivities, collective and personal identities, and the politics of aesthetics that emerge around self-representation and trauma" (48). *Stolen Life* lives up to Gilmore's assessment, generating dialogue about the "politics of aesthetics" surrounding this text's representation of trauma and the self constituted by that trauma. To what extent does *Stolen Life* live up to Gilmore's appraisal of limit-cases as authoring "representations of the self and trauma that refuse the deformations of legalistic demands" (44)? Although Johnson turns away from a legal medium, her account inevitably addresses a system that, she and Wiebe maintain, denied her justice. Johnson, however, never directly appeals to this system in her testimony; rather, it is Wiebe who represents her in the three chapters sorting through the legal proceedings of her case. Johnson instead appeals to the reader in a telling that emphasizes her healing, in a context removed from her legal incrimination. When she does come forth with her confession, she situates it in a strictly spiritual context. Collaborative authorship creates the opportunity for these split discursive registers, permitting Wiebe to address the law while Johnson addresses her interlocutor, her reader and, in her diary entries, herself in a discourse that is primarily therapeutic. Johnson and Wiebe manage the narrative in a way that allows her to circumvent the constraints the law places on self-representation. In doing so, they successfully structure an alternative hearing, one that resists legal scrutiny and the singular judgment it imparts.

Notes

1 When asked about his reasons for advising Johnson not to testify, Johnson's lawyer Brian Beresh explains that it is customary to keep the accused from testifying in cases where two stand charged with the crime so that their testimonies cannot be used against each other. Following this explanation, however, Beresh provides further reasoning supporting his decision. He tells Wiebe, "'Yvonne does not present well, [she] does not look too good'" (318).
2 *Oxford English Dictionary*, 2nd ed., s.v. "testimony."
3 See, for instance, Bird, Fast, and Beard.
4 See Friedberg.
5 Formed by 1986 in Toronto by Lenore Keeshig-Tobias, Tomson Highway, and Daniel David Moses. The CRET's aim was, in Keeshig-Tobia's summary, "to consolidate and gain recognition for Native contributions to Canadian writing—to reclaim the Native voice in literature" (1988, 3). This political and cultural mandate was carried out through the publication of *The Magazine to Re-establish the Trickster*, as well as seminars, performances, and workshops.

6 Located in Penticton, British Columbia, and directed by Jeannette Armstrong, the En'owkin School of Writing offers a creative writing program for Native writers.

7 Part of Johnson's inheritance, Wiebe observes, is exteriorized, shared with her maternal grandmother, Flora Bear, who "passed on to her [...] her own manifest gift of a cleft palate" (436). Johnson similarly writes in a letter to Wiebe: *"A bear always has a fold in her upper lip. My grandma, I, my eldest child, have the gift and the legacy of the bear so strong, we have the Bear's Lip"* (436; italics in original).

8 Johnson's involuntary transfer to the Edmonton Institute for Women occurred in 2001. She was initially transferred to the Regional Psychiatric Centre (RPC) in Saskatoon, a medium–maximum security institution that functions as both a penitentiary and psychiatric facility. Critics of this institution argue that it is worse than a prison because of its limited programs and exemption from provisions in the CCRA (Corrections and Conditional Release Act), the legislation that regulates the imprisonment and release of federally sentenced prisoners. Discrepancies exist between the CCRA and Saskatchewan's Mental Health Act, the two legislative acts that preside over the operation of RPC. For instance, the RPC makes participation in therapy compulsory for inmates, while the CCRA provides no legal authority to force therapy on inmates without their consent. The facility's "treatment" and "security" mandates contradict each another and lead to violations of the patient/prisoner's rights. See Thomas. Subsequent to her transfer to RPC, Johnson was moved to the Edmonton Institute for Women.

9 Egan borrows this term from Suzette Henke, who describes scriptotherapy as "the process of writing out and writing through traumatic experience in the mode of therapeutic reenactment" (xii). "Through the artistic replication of a coherent subject-position," she formulates, "the life-writing project generates a healing narrative that temporarily restores the fragmented self to an empowered position of psychological agency" (xvi).

FOUR Prison Collections and Periodicals

In an illuminating survey of the penal press in Canada, criminologist Robert Gaucher points out the "dearth of available documentation which provides an account of the experiences of criminalization and incarceration from the perspective of those subjected to it" ("Canadian Penal Press" 3). Gaucher performs his own inaugural work as he compiles a history of penal publications from the 1950s to the present. His scholarship confronts the difficulty of accessing many of the publications originating from the prison, but it also underlines the special difficulties encountered by the publications he collates: "Confined by the isolation of incarceration, faced with the prospect of pleasing both administration and fellow prisoners, constrained by the often unintelligible censorship demands [...] editors ha[ve] to walk a tightrope of conflicting demands and expectations in a situation where failure could have serious consequences" (7). Gaucher describes these challenges as an inexorable part of editing "joint" magazines. Al Sinobert identifies a similar set of obstacles in his editorial statement to *Tribal Ways*, a publication from Collins Bay Institution: "There are a number of problems when doing a paper from within the walls of a prison. One cannot be critical of the institutional policies, or criticize the penal system in general. One cannot single-out and criticize any police agency, politician, social agency, or any religious sector. So one is left with the idea of expressing the bitterness and general observations of social interaction of society [...] or the injustice of the courts toward native people [o]r expressions of feeling and thoughts before and while incarcerated" (n.p.).

The challenges Sinobert notes can prohibit prisoners' expression. The inside cover of a 1991 issue of *Tightwire* provides a concrete example of the restrictions—here in the form of institutional censorship—that Gaucher and Sinobert describe. Still visible on close scrutiny, the deleted text disparages prison staff and incites resistance and rioting among female inmates. This example draws attention to post-publication interventions that take place as the writing is filtered through the "concrete curtain" (Guiney 5).

The title of the publication cited above, *Tightwire*, returns us to the different audience demands that Gaucher outlines. Prison writer Gregory McMaster treats the question of audience as the quandary of the prison writer generally: "The constant dilemma faced by any prison writer is how to effectively educate and inform the public about the realities of our lives without insulting and alienating the very people we are trying to help? We become tightrope walkers, forever walking the fine line in our attempts to articulate the facts without ostracizing our fellow prisoners" (51).

This point of audience is central to any study of prison writing: it figures not just in the prewriting process—in the community the inmate author seeks—but also in the writing itself. What readership do prison writers envision in their "act of personal liberation" (Bruchac, "Breaking Out" 289)? Frank Guiney argues that prison literature—specifically, the "convict poetry" and "jailhouse ballads" that characterized an older prison tradition before the 1950s—was once "in every sense a truly 'inside' culture medium" (3). He explains:

> It was written only for other convicts. Seldom did the "square-John," the outsider, encounter a real jailhouse poem; and if he did, he could rarely feel or fully comprehend its impact, because the experience of the poem could not possibly relate to anything within his frame of reference. Convict irony and convict humour would go over his head; and convict sensibility would fail to penetrate his heart. The joke, the tragedy, the understanding, was ours alone, written between the lines, unspoken, sub-surfaced—much in the style we lived our lives; much like the expressionless faces we showed to our keepers.
>
> What outsider could fully understand! (3)

Guiney goes on to identify a shift—concurrent with the advent of the penal press in the 1950s—in which prison writing came to be read by a non-imprisoned public. As a result, the "scope" of prison writing "has widened, taken on a new tone," Guiney observes. "And it may be that outsiders understand more and listen a bit closer and care a little" (5–6). But its tenor, he insists, can only be fully understood by those who have been there.

A great deal of the writing in prison serials is specific in its content and imagined audience. For instance, "The Four Seasons of Prison," by P4W inmate T.A. Glaremin, is an extended reflection on inmates' removal from the natural rhythms of day and night and the cycles of the seasons. The women experience the seasons only indirectly; the spring "rains that echo from the concrete" are faint reminders of the innocence and renewal these cycles once signalled (8). Winter brings the "voices of dead sisters" (6); autumn leaves the women "deadened to the long winter ahead" (12). Even summer, the most revitalizing of all the seasons, takes on destructive dimensions that reflect the extent of the inmates' deprivation: "When Summer comes, we burn our bodies—nude in the sun—in the prison yard, / hoping to die by nature, than by our own hands" (10–11). Like the morning light that "floods our floors with artificial hope" (5), the seasons are transmuted, skewed, and ominous as they are experienced from behind the prison walls. The poem ends: "Darkness never comes in prison, until they cut us down and carefully lay us in a body / bag. Then the CSC turn the night lights off" (15–17). Despite their best wishes, the women end up dying by their own hands: the final image is of their hanging.

Glaremin's poem depicts the prison through a series of negations and absences. The four seasons evoke not renewal for the female prisoners but death. While resemblances might be drawn between this experience and the "modern" condition depicted in *The Waste Land*, this experience takes on more concrete and claustrophobic dimensions than its diffuse and subjective rendering in Eliot's work. Deprived of the natural rhythms of the seasons, the prisoners' limited enjoyment of them takes on a violent edge. Those fleeting elements of nature that do enter the space of the prison— the rains echoing through the concrete walls or the diffused morning light—are altered, estranged from how they are experienced on the outside. Even the women's inevitable death is estranged from its natural dimensions; the poet describes their death as CSC turning out the night lights of the prison. In such a denaturalized environment, hope also becomes "artificial." This poem's meaning is not inaccessible to a non-prisoner or outsider; it does, though, detail, painfully and lyrically, an experience few can understand. The poem's oxymoronic title, "The Four Seasons of Prison," cues this separation, drawing attention to the specificity of place and its inalienable experiences.

Women in Cages: Gender and the Formation of Community

Glaremin's "Four Seasons of Prison" gestures toward a female prisoner community and reminds us of the role that gender, as well as race, plays in these authors' writing and sense of audience. Considering that women, and more particularly, "poor, young, racialized women [...] are among the fastest growing prison populations in Canada and worldwide," as Lisa Neve and Kim Pate point out, the voices of women prisoners are becoming more insistent (19).[1] Yet scholarship on prison writing has more often focused on male subjects. Past scholarly works, when they address women's prison writing at all, focus on individuals who are part of revolutionary movements. Recent critical studies by Judith Scheffler attempt to redress the scarcity of attention paid to "firsthand accounts by poor and working-class imprisoned women" (*Wall Tappings* xvii). Scheffler illuminates the specific problems articulated by women prisoners, such as their difficult separation from their children. She joins Sharon Hileman in further noting an increasing emphasis on community in women's prison writing, often visible in the collaborative nature of women's prison texts. "The Four Seasons of Prison" describes the prison as female subjects experience it. When read beside the writing of other female prisoners published in prison periodicals, this poem becomes a recognizable lament for those who have died in prison—an elegy for dead sisters, as well as for those like the speaker who, while not yet dead, experience a slow death in this place. A lyrical poem spoken in the collective "we" and elegizing a collective death, this poem provides an example of a unique autobiographical discourse emerging from prison.

Other female prison authors refer to this idea of sisterhood and thereby encourage a reading of the prison through the lens of gender. "For Strong Women," a poem by an author named Blue that appeared in P4W's *Tightwire*, posits a female community in its content, context of publication, and audience. The author's dedication, "to my very special sisters in the Hole," combined with the title, "For Strong Women," suggests a female prisoner audience. The poem begins by reciting a series of insufferable tasks. "A strong woman," the poem opens, is "a woman who is / straining" (1–2). As she shovels, she

> talks about how she doesn't mind
> crying, it opens up the ducts of the
> eyes, and throwing up develops the
> stomach muscles, and she goes on
> shoveling with tears in her nose. (9–13)

The poem emphasizes an unflagging mental fortitude with which the female subject performs these acts of drudgery. The quiet resilience she maintains in the face of degradation is further reinforced with the entry of a male figure in the poem. "A strong woman," the poem proceeds to describe,

> is a woman in whose
> head is repeating, I told
> you so, ugly girl bad girl, bitch,
> nag, shrill witch, ballbuster (14–17)

The invective continues in the lines

> nobody will ever love you back, why
> aren't you feminine, why aren't you
> soft, [w]hy aren't you quiet, why
> aren't you dead? (18–21)

The references to "feminine," "quiet," and "dead" urge a passivity that contrasts with the portrait of a "strong woman" in the previous lines. The gender-motivated violence visited on the female subject thus creates another dimension to her denigration. Detailing experiences shared by the women in this environment, the poem implicitly puts forth a women's community. "Strong / is what we make each other," the speaker affirms near the end of the poem (63–64). In the specificity of the experiences it depicts, this poem points to crucial differences that again present the need to nuance prison communities along lines of gender.

The problems unique to female Aboriginal prisoners are also the subject of Ms. Cree's "Entrenched Social Catastrophe," an expository piece that first appeared in *Tightwire*.[2] This essay addresses class, economic, and racial issues that, together, contribute to Aboriginal women's subjugate social position and mistreatment by the justice system. Their systemic and institutional violation persists, the author writes, "1) because we are women; 2) we are Native; 3) we are poor; and 4) we do not usually possess an education equivalent to the status quo" (45). Raising the specific set of challenges that Aboriginal women endure within the justice and correctional system, the author speaks on behalf of an inmate community that is both indigenous and female. Indeed, the author maintains that her subject position exceeds that of a female inmate community. "I am your typical Native woman," she ends—a self-conception further implied in her pseudonym, Ms. Cree. Casting herself as representative of Aboriginal women, in her essay she diminishes any distinctions between indigenous women outside the prison and those within it.

"Entrenched Social Catastrophe" combines different rhetorical styles to render, from the vantage point of an Aboriginal female inmate, the experience of prison life. The author explores how Aboriginal women offenders are misperceived by the criminal justice system. She prefaces the work by arguing that Aboriginal people "are more likely to be 'gated' under The Dangerous Offenders Act, Bills C-67 and C-68, and therefore deemed the most dangerous and most violent offenders in Canada" (45). This is most often the case for Aboriginal women because of the specific type of discrimination they experience while in the prison system. The author then proceeds to mimic her institutional profile as it would be written up by a parole caseworker. The profile depersonalizes the author, providing a summary of her infractions. In his preface to the American prisoners' anthology, *Words from the House of the Dead*, editor Bill Witherup explains the particular discourse of the inmate's file: "Everything in prison is structured on a negative basis. A man's file, his jacket, which is usually the basis of his parole, contains mostly negative information, infractions of the rules. Your persona is a negative one the moment you set foot in the prison" (n.p.). Ms. Cree's mimicry of her institutional profile effectively demonstrates how Aboriginal inmates are viewed by parole workers and subsequently denied re-entry into society. After this "fictional profile," she describes in a more personal tone what it is like to suffer through the deadening monotony of the prison. Her detailed summary of the kind of violence and manipulation endured by female inmates in this environment draws attention to the omissions and silences of her institutional profile. "We adjust to increasingly deadly conditions, and come to accept them as 'natural,'" she explains (46). "We have adjusted to the deafening noises and screams coming from segregation when our Sister has just been stripped of her clothes and maced in the face" (46). An acerbic humour laces some of her later descriptions of the absurd dimensions their lives take on in this setting. These descriptions provide an incisive glimpse of the deadening, insanity-inducing conditions of prison life. Together with her mock institutional profile, the author's arguments undermine her characterization by the prison bureaucracy and challenge the legislative powers that continue to entrench this social catastrophe.

These three works drawn from *Tightwire* demonstrate the discursive character of writing published in "joint magazines" and the types of rhetorical strategies used by authors writing about this setting. While D. Quentin Miller claims that "prison narratives are written primarily (even exclusively) for outsiders, not for inmates" (15), many of the works in these prison serials unravel Miller's assumption about the primary reader envisioned by this writing. The audience of these works consists primarily of a prisoner readership. Addressing a specifically female community, the authors reveal a conception of audience that is influenced by their institutional setting, and in particular by the gender segregation of the prison.

These prison magazines function as venues of community where the writer sounds a voice on behalf of her fellow prisoners. In "Entrenched Social Catastrophe," the author treats the plight of the Aboriginal female prisoner as that of Aboriginal women generally. Her conception of audience extends beyond the prison, but not in the way that Miller imagines; the prison becomes, rather, an emblem of the specific social and economic restrictions experienced by indigenous women. While revealing the role that institutions play in community formation, these writings depict such communities as a nexus of support and resistance. These works further show the generic diversity of writing from prison, a diversity that arguably defies the idea of prison writing as a genre. In the changing space of the prison, how might the writing of Aboriginal women reflect different concerns and an altogether different writing praxis? These works reveal how the thematics of the prison text may take on different contours in the hands of female authors. A similar focus on audience and on the generic diversity of this writing follows my discussion of the oral forms adapted by writers in prison.

Oral Cultures in the Prison

Prison authors engage various genres in writing about the prison; some of these genres include oral forms. In each of the texts discussed so far, writing is an important act of liberation, a means for the author to transcend his/her physical confinement by establishing a dialogue with an outside community. Critics of prison writing, however, have frequently remarked on a rich and varied oral culture of the prison, citing for instance the prison's particular vocabulary or "con-lingo." In his essay "Prison Slang and the Poetics of Imprisonment," Douglas Taylor notes: "From the prison work songs and blues tunes sung by convicts in the first half of the twentieth century to the complex linguistic codes that circulate within prison walls today, orality has always been an important part of prison culture" (233). Incarcerated Canadian author Frank Guiney further describes the subterranean development of a prison oral culture:

> Surreptitious in its conception, and furtive in its lifetime, this bit of underground culture functioned quietly for decades behind the grey walls, spreading from cell to cell, from block to block and from memory to memory by whispered word of mouth. It was a smidgeon of free expression, a part of man that cannot be contained by shackles and bars and concrete; it was a bit of feeling, a scrap of humour, a little release that could not be stifled by the rules and regulations and punishments and deprivations of a caged world. (3)

The type of creation Guiney describes is a collective utterance, a form of expression conceived not in singularity, but in a type of quiet collectivity. Gaucher notes the endurance of these oral forms in contemporary prisons. "Prison culture," he observes, "is still characterized by an oral tradition of songs and ballads, storytelling and 'dead time' conversations" ("Canadian Penal Press" 14). Guiney and Gaucher both cite the jailhouse ballad as an instance of such a tradition. These ballads were passed down orally and, Guiney points out, often made their way into sweatshops and work gangs. The diffusion of the jailhouse ballad that Guiney describes draws attention to the cross-pollination of discursive forms and to the permeable boundaries between imprisoned populations and "free" ones.

Though the oral culture discussed by Guiney and Gaucher provides a context for reading the prison texts in this chapter, situating this consideration within critical scholarship on indigenous literature is crucial to understanding the oral traditions adapted by Aboriginal prison authors. All prisons have an oral culture; Aboriginal prisoners stand in special relation to such oral life. The continuation of oral traditions in contemporary indigenous literature is a frequently noted characteristic of this writing. Thomas King refers to this blending of oral and written forms as "interfusional literature," a practice that draws on some of the structures, tropes, and syntax of oral literature but reproduces these in written form (13). Catherine Rainwater observes the power of oral storytelling to intervene in dominant discourses and narratives, an observation echoed by other critics. In his discussion of orally narrated autobiographies, David Brumble remarks that "even embedded [...] in written words, in books, these oral traditions have still the power to struggle against the conventions of the dominant culture" (46–47). The resistive potential of oral forms invites us to recognize the oral traditions that appear in the writing of Aboriginal prisoners as contributing to another register of meaning. In the literature examined in this discussion, traditional, indigenous narratives supplement the prison lore of tall tales and stories about life, crime, and punishment historically associated with the prison. What role or special function does the incorporation of Aboriginal oral traditions have in the contexts of the prison and its literature?

The oral traditions found in this writing could be viewed, on one hand, as evidence of cultural continuance and adaptability. In "Coming Home Through Stories," Cree scholar Neal McLeod formulates the value of storytelling for cultures that have experienced the colonizing effects of diaspora and exile. His discussion has an obvious resonance for a prison context: "The process of diaspora involves both physical and spiritual enclosement. It is a move away from the familiar towards a new alien 'space.' This new space attempts to transform and mutate pre-existing narratives and social structures" (28). The prison represents an extreme form of the historical experience McLeod describes. Story, McLeod argues, is a way of retaining a sense of identity and belonging in the midst of the experience of exile. McLeod cites as his example stories told after ê-mây-ihkamikahk, or "where it went wrong" (The Northwest Resistance). He goes on to show how this historical experience "and the trauma associated with it are manifested in the stories told" (31). He makes a compelling case for the manner in which stories reflect the circumstances of their telling. Their power to "negotiate through the field of experience" (28) renders them a valuable discursive form for Aboriginal inmates, whose incarceration is part of the larger, collective experience McLeod discusses.

Given the high concentration of Aboriginal inmates, the prison often provides the possibility of reconnecting with one's cultural traditions. Many prisoners are reintroduced to traditional stories while in prison, by Elder-mentors and possibly by other inmates. In the manner that McLeod describes, oral storytelling would play a crucial part in this reconnection. Somewhat related to this topic, Margery Fee proposes that the integration of oral modes in Aboriginal writing—the insertion of "textual markers of orality" and a writer who "takes on the mantle of the oral story-teller" ("Writing Orality" 24)—may function as a way of countering cultural loss and the erosion of indigenous languages. In these works, one witnesses a revival of oral forms and a creative mingling of expressive traditions where indigenous cultural forms are brought back into the mix.

In "Aboriginal Text in Context," Greg Young-Ing writes: "Aboriginal Peoples found ways to incorporate traditional institutions and aspects of culture with new mediums into the contemporary context [...] [They] have shown through their adaptation that their dynamic cultures do not remain encapsulated in the past, static, and resistant to development" (237–38). The reworking of oral modes into writing is part of the adaptation that Young-Ing emphasizes. The value of traditional oral narratives to prison literature is in their ability to speak to the experiences of their teller and audience, to provide a social framework for communicating individual experiences. In "The Raven," a traditional story by "C. Cassil" in Words from Inside, the resourcefulness and guile exercised by the trickster contribute to a subtext of resistance. This register of struggle and hard-won triumph might have special appeal to a prisoner audience constrained by its own set of physical and ideological restrictions. In a similar allegorical manner, two traditional narratives that appear at the beginning and end of Native Sons—Ron Cooper's introductory story and a concluding narrative titled "The Loon and the Blind Man"—establish a frame for reading the collection. As self-reflexive devices, these stories function as guides for approaching the prisoners' stories and poetry in the collection. The audience for *Native Sons* includes imprisoned and non-imprisoned readers, both Aboriginal and non-Aboriginal. Other works, like "Ballad of Ron Cooper" and the trickster story from *Words from Inside,* appear to be geared more toward an Aboriginal prisoner community. In each instance the traditional oral performance of these stories serves as an emblem of the interaction between the storyteller and reader.

Trickster in the Prison

A trickster tale from *Words from Inside* titled "The Raven" illustrates the translatable power of the trickster within a prison setting. Translated from Tlingit, the story opens with a description of Raven's significance: "Raven, this cultural hero—transformer—trickster, perhaps the oldest strata of myth in the Native Mythology, was born the son of a proud father who taught him in the ways of subterfuge and gave him strength, strength to make a world, a task in which he succeeded ingeniously" (6). Raven's trickery here has collective consequences; his resourcefulness is not for individual benefit but with the result of "mak[ing] a world" (6). Raven's altruistic motives in this telling contrast with another version of the story recorded by Bill Reid and Robert Bringhurst. In the Reid and Bringhurst version, Raven acts out of acquisitiveness and self-interest, unlike this Raven, whose intentions are nobler. Raven emerges in this narrative as a Prometheus figure who brings light, the stars, and the moon to the rest of the world. The portentous language describing Raven's great deed further creates overtones of Genesis in this story.

Until Raven's interventions, light and the heavenly bodies remain the sole possession of a rich and selfish old man who lives with his beautiful daughter. In a scheme to "bestow onto mankind the benefits of this light" (6), Raven shapeshifts into a piece of dirt and conceals himself in a drinking vessel. The daughter becomes impregnated when she drinks from the container, and Raven is born as her child. Soon after the child learns to crawl, Raven entreats the old man to give him the bundles of stars and moon on the walls. With the last bundle safely in his hand, the child "utter[s] the Raven cry—'Gaaa'—and fl[ies] out with it through the smoke hole," releasing light into the world (7). Too late in realizing his deception, the old man reacts with anger and curses Raven (7). This story reinforces the potential for gain in a situation of disadvantage. A redistribution of resources takes place for the use of others. Unlike the version recorded by Reid and Bringhurst, in which the animals are the main beneficiaries of Raven's actions, this story does not specify whether humans or animals benefit more greatly. These differences point to the situational aspect of storytelling. By keeping the beneficiaries of Raven's interventions unspecified, this story includes a human community and possibly allows a prison audience to identify with the story's content. "The Raven" depicts an act of liberation from and a mastery over a controlling force. In this story, the trickster's scheming has powerful, dramatic consequences. Neal McLeod interestingly remarks that trickster stories were often told for the purpose of "transform[ing] the circumstances that the people were living in" (21–22). It is reasonable to imagine the allure that the trickster, a figure who uses mental cunning and resourcefulness to outwit those more powerful than himself, would have for a prisoner audience. The limited opportunity for expression in the prison creates the necessary conditions for the allegorical subtext of these trickster stories to resonate.

Within a prison setting, one could expect an element of prefiguration to these traditional stories—that the audience, in Karl Kroeber's description, enters "a familiar telling" (32). Prefiguration is a component of oral storytelling in which "the important portion of a tale's audience already knows the story. For them and anyone who returns to a narrative, prefiguration takes account of this foreknowledge [...] Prefiguring allows the imagination of informed listeners to reshape what has, for them, already happened at least once" (32). Kroeber's reference to the "important portion of a tale's audience" implies an audience in the know. His formulation of prefiguration is continuous with Guiney's discussion of "insider" stories, in which the prisoner audience, already versed in the narrative, proleptically awaits an expected outcome. In this story, this presumed audience is conceivably an imprisoned community. It may also be an Aboriginal reading audience generally that is just as likely to be familiar with the conventions of trickster stories. A process in which the listener's experience is guided by foreknowledge of how the story will unfold, prefiguration invites both teller and listener to "reshape" the narrative and adapt it to their contexts. The elements of the story do not necessarily change; rather, their framing does. The traditional oral narration of these stories remains in the background as a reminder of their performance and of the audience's role in the shifting meanings of the story. This type of interaction continues in the tradition of oral storytelling. As anthropologists, literary critics, and authors themselves have frequently pointed out, tellers imprint themselves on their stories, sometimes even autobiographically.[3] Narrators may also select the content of the story according to their listeners' identities. This trickster story invites us to recognize the interpersonal transactions that occur in the context of storytelling and how the author's experiences influence the resultant narrative.

Traditional Stories as Allegories of Reading

The allegorical behaviour of traditional stories extends beyond the themes of resistance seen in the trickster story above. The two stories that begin and end *Native Sons* self-reflexively establish a frame for reading the collection by functioning as commentaries on the reader's interaction with the text. Ron Cooper's introduction opens: *"Once in a while there comes along a book that has a certain kind of reading. This is such a book. In fact it brought back to my mind the story of a special bullet"* (n.p.; italics Cooper's). This "certain kind of reading" triggers a story about a hunter who embarks on a desperate search for food. With one remaining bullet in his gun, he takes his chances on a partridge that he encounters as he is about to give up. When the struck partridge falls to the ground, it scares a nearby moose. The moose, in turn, falls over a small cliff. Astonished by his good fortune, the hunter arrives to clean the moose and discovers, to his further surprise, a silver fox beneath it. The story closes with the following statement: *"The essence of this story you will find in this book. It has been put together by a few Indians, who have used their time with creative tempo, to express their personal feelings on life and how they see it from the steel bars of man"* (n.p.; italics Cooper's).

What purpose would this narrative serve at the beginning of the collection? Saying that the story's meaning can be found in the following pages suspends the act of interpretation until the reader's encounter with the remainder of the text. The silver bullet story thus frames the reading of the collection, urging the reader to take chances in his/her reading, to suspend judgment for the possibility of finding something that may not be apparent. A similar metaphor for reading this text can be found in the last work of the collection, a short story titled "The Loon and the Blind Man." In this tale, a hungry old man sets out fishing. After several hours without a bite, he refuses to give up and becomes blind from the burning reflection of the sun on the water. Desperate, the old man calls out for help and attracts the attention of a loon. Instructing the old man to hold on to its body, the loon plunges into the water and surfaces with a sturgeon each time he dives. The water soothes the old man's eyes until he regains his sight. His vision restored, the old man thanks the loon gratefully. At their parting, the loon offers two fish to the old man, and the old man, in return, gives the loon a necklace of white shells.

"The Loon and the Blind Man" reinforces the idea of something restorative existing beneath the immediate surface. Placing too much confidence in appearances, this story suggests, can be blinding. Also central to this narrative is the theme of exchange, both in the loon's offering of assistance to the old man and in their gifts to each other at their parting. This exchange, which could be seen as a metaphor for the transaction between the reader and the author, is connected to the story's message of reaching outside oneself or one's realm of familiarity.

As metaphors for the reader's interpretive engagement with this writing, these traditional stories serve as appropriate bookends for this collection of poetry and short stories. "Retold," "translated," or "brought back to mind" by the occasion of the telling, these stories are adapted and performed. This sense of performance is a vestige of their oral tradition and comes to frame the stories metanarratively. "Performance," notes Richard Bauman, "sets up, or represents, an interpretive frame within which the messages being communicated are to be understood" (9). In their textual reproduction, these stories shift their model of interaction from what were once teller and listener to what are now author and reader. These stories demonstrate a flexibility by speaking both to the author's immediate prison context and to the context of reading. Prison writing, this study repeatedly emphasizes, is crucially about establishing a dialogue. The two stories that open and conclude *Native Sons* establish the nature of this dialogue, define the spirit of the reading that takes place.

Crossed Traditions: "Ballad of Ron Cooper"

"Ballad of Ron Cooper," a poem by Ray Nobis Jr. in *Native Sons*, brings together the prison folk ballad with a model of individual reformation. The subject of this poem is the spiritual recovery of Ron Cooper, who is himself a contributor to the collection. The portrayal of Ron Cooper in the first half of the poem draws on conventions of the prison ballad Guiney discusses. Noted first for his infamy, as a "brother of hell" who grew up "hard and mean" (8–9), this outlaw figure inspires both fear and awe. Described as "Half-Indian and half animal" (10), he becomes caged in a "six by nine foot cell" (13). Ron Cooper's legendary status derives from the "hundred lives" he has lived, the peril he has survived (2). Like the jailhouse ballad, which is often noted for its "bitter and mean" tone (Guiney 3), this poem centres on a subject who embodies these qualities in a superlative sense. "Ballad of Ron Cooper" resembles the prison folk ballad in form as well as content. With a semi-regular rhyme pattern and insertions like "so the story goes" (14), this poem unfolds much like an oral ballad. "He's like a history book" (44), this poem remarks of its hero—a description that reaffirms Bruchac's earlier treatment of these creations as oral prison history.

The hero's "half-Indian and half animal" status also calls attention to the hybridity of this poetic creation—to its crossed influences. Midway into the poem, Ron Cooper undergoes a transformation. Over twenty-five years of jail time turns this dispassionate, hardened individual into a man who realizes "he just wanted to be free" (25). His transformation comes about as he reconnects with "The Sacred Hoop," the spiritual teachings of his indigenous heritage (31). The grave mood of the first half lifts as the poem describes the restoration of spiritual values. The rhyme structure begins to loosen at this point and dissolves altogether in the last eleven lines, which affirm Ron Cooper's spiritual rebirth. He becomes "wise, witty and happy," a man who "can now see brighter days" (37–38). From a legend whose past was so hard it "might seem untrue" (5), Ron Cooper emerges as a "simple man, just like you and me" (48). In this divided portrait can be seen the two influences of this poem. One of these is the prison ballad, which typically centres on an individual whose life is exemplary. Ron Cooper's portrait adheres to this tradition in the first half of the poem, where it is his "dark and hateful" (4) past and twenty-five years of prison time that provide the central focus. The latter part of the poem centres on Ron Cooper's transformation and significance as a spiritual mentor. By the end of the poem it is his "representativeness" rather than his legendary status that inspires his poetic exaltation. The "hundred lives" he has lived shift to suggest those lives that resemble his own.

The spiritual transformation that this poem charts reflects a relatively recent prison consciousness influenced by the resurgence of indigenous teachings in Canadian prisons. Led by individuals like Art Solomon, this movement produced Native Brotherhood and Sisterhood organizations and earned recognition for the practice of indigenous spiritual rituals as fundamental prisoners' rights. Solomon's *Eating Bitterness: A Vision Beyond the Prison Walls* is a collection of poems, essays, and speeches that offers both a critique of the Canadian justice system and a model for travelling the "Good Red Road" (Rarihokwats n.p.). "Ballad of Ron Cooper" brings this emergent prison sensibility into dialogue with an older prison folk tradition. The individual moral and spiritual restoration depicted in this poem marks a parallel or an alternative to the type of religious conversion often found in prison writing.

The oral forms employed in these works function, then, in a number of ways—as a means of merging a prison oral tradition with indigenous oral traditions and as allegories of resistance and reading. Oral culture infuses this literature from two sources: from the different forms circulating throughout "cellblock country" and from the oral traditions belonging to Aboriginal cultures. "Ballad of Ron Cooper" provides an example of the meeting of these two influences and thus attests to the dialogues among different discursive traditions in the prison. In the trickster story from *Words from Inside*, a prisoner audience's interaction with the narrative forms a subtext to the telling: the trickster's clever interventions and ability to outwit those more powerful than himself would resonate strongly within a prison setting. In the two traditional stories that frame *Native Sons*, it is an outside audience's engagement with this writing that enters into their meaning and their metaphorical operation. With this chapter, then, I have returned to some of the central considerations visited throughout this study: the discursive strategies used by prison authors, the generic and formal variety of this writing, the different communities negotiated in this literature, and the types of reading it asks of its audience. Positioned in unique relation to the prison, these writers engage with existing prison forms in ways that reflect their cultural traditions, their historically charged relationship to this structure, and their experience within this institution as one of resistance rather than "rehabilitation."

Notes

1 Aboriginal women constitute roughly 30 percent of the female prisoner population, though they make up only 2 percent of the general national population (Statistics Canada 16). In Saskatchewan and Manitoba, they account for roughly 85 percent of all female admissions (Statistics Canada 18).

2 First published in *Tightwire* 20, no. 4 (26–28). The passages cited are from its subsequent publication in *Journal of Prisoners on Prison*.

3 See, for instance, Julie Cruikshank, Kathleen Mullen Sands, and Theodore Rios.

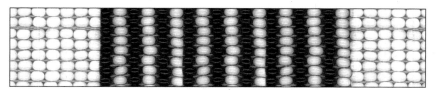

PART TWO Genre in the Institutional Setting of the Residential School

The movement from prison writing to residential school accounts is premised on the proximate place these two structures occupy in the carceral continuum sketched out in the introduction. Together, these two bodies of literature constitute a larger category of "carceral writing"—works written from the carceral spaces of the prison and residential school. In Foucault's paradigm, the prison is part of a larger gradation of mechanisms of control, a relay of power that "move[s] gradually from the correction of irregularities to the punishment of crime" (299). Quite within the vein of Foucault's theories, the authors in this second half of the book note similarities between the prison and the residential school, pointing to their mutual function in a larger carceral network.

One might be compelled to make an immediate distinction, however, between the mass institutionalization of Aboriginal children and the more individualized process of incrimination experienced by the authors in the previous chapters. That is, while the former were placed in residential schools heedless of any infraction or attribution of "guilt," the latter were incarcerated on the basis of individual transgression. Yet guilt also figures in the residential school experience: students were made to feel guilty simply for who they were. This inherent guilt is pointed out by Leonard Peltier as he speaks about his experience at Wahpeton Boarding School, and also by James Tyman in his impressions of the Aboriginal children at the Lebret Residential School. A precondition of this form of institutional containment, guilt becomes a significant consideration for the authors writing from this different, but homologous, setting. The prison writers and residential school authors in this study indicate that guilt is not necessarily correlated with criminality. As the works in this section show, guilt can be imposed on an individual or individuals who have committed no crime. The previous chapters indicate, as well, that one can be convicted of a crime of which one is innocent. Moreover, in instances where a crime has been committed, that person may reconcile feelings of personal culpability and shed his/her sense of institutional guilt.

Certain distinctions exist between the type of guilt attributed to the imprisoned authors in Part One and the child subjects of this chapter; even so, the similarities between the two are worth considering. Mi'kmaq author Isabelle Knockwood makes a revealing comparison between the residential school and the prison in *Out of the Depths*, her account of the Shubenacadie Residential School. The very name of the school, she remarks, evoked associations with miscreants and criminals. "'Don't do that or you'll be sent to Shubie,' was a standard threat to children," Knockwood recalls. "The school was so strongly associated with punishment in children's minds that those who were 'sent to Shubie' as a result of their family's circumstances constantly wondered what crime they had committed" (86). Knockwood's statements call attention to economic factors (by "family's circumstances" Knockwood means those parents who could not show economic means to prove their fitness as a family, and so were compelled to send their children earlier than required by the law), while also underscoring the school's association with punishment.

If students were unfamiliar with this allocation of guilt before entering the residential school, they encountered it early into their time there. At several points in her residential school autobiography, Jane Willis describes the staff's condemnation of the girls for sexual promiscuity— charges that are unfounded. So absurd are these allusions to sexual indecency that the girls do not initially grasp the meaning behind the warnings. Once they come to understand the behaviour of which the staff suggest they are guilty, Willis and her classmates eventually give up disputing the validity of such claims, realizing that there is no way for them to prove their innocence in this system where their guilt is preassigned. In almost all of the texts examined in Part Two of this book, the religious teachings of the residential school play a primary role in the process of guilt acquisition. These teachings quite often instilled a type of guilt—in Peltier's terms, "Aboriginal Sin"—predicated on race. The prison evolved from the belief that the individual's removal could be a means of spiritual and moral transformation; the residential school functioned as a similar place of containment and hoped-for conversion and absorption into "normative," dominant culture.

The authors in the following chapters resist this process of conversion. Their texts assert an independent consciousness that defies the residential school's control. Given that a great part of this resistance is waged at the level of the writing, a significant consideration is the type of genre each writer takes up to inscribe his/her experience in this setting. Testimony will remain relevant in this section, though in its broader sense of bearing witness to individual and collective trauma. These works' engagements with history are also part of their function as testimonies. Confession, a mode of discourse that figured prevalently in the writings of condemned authors, will play a less important role here. This half of the book will see the appearance of new genres to this study—memoir and the novel—that will enrich its investigation of form. What is the relation between genre and content in these texts, and what might an author's use of genre reveal about the level of resistance in the narrative? To what extent do these authors uphold or push the conventions of the genres they engage? What may genre tell us that the narrative may not?

This part of the book will take up these questions with an examination of five texts written about the authors' residential school experiences. My discussion begins with Basil Johnston's memoir *Indian School Days*. I will consider the relation between Johnston's institutional setting and the type of writing he chooses for writing about his residential school experience. Johnston's effort to efface his centrality in the narrative and to cast himself as one of an entire dramatis personae is both a typical manoeuvre of the memoir writer and a significant component of the group solidarity at the centre of his text. The recession of the writing subject from the narrative further contributes to this text's act of collective witnessing. Similarly, Johnston's extensive description of his classmates' roguish behaviour is part of this text's countering of tragic chronicles of post-contact indigenous life. These characteristics of Johnston's memoir combine to construct a shared history, playfully and fondly retold, out of a repressive environment that might have been expected to create a sense of fragmentation.

A similar narrative playfulness characterizes Tomson Highway's autobiographical novel *Kiss of the Fur Queen*. This text uses humour to deflate the language of religion, the institutional discourse against which

Highway writes. Like the antics that dominate Johnston's narrative, the trickster's comic entry into this text is part of the undoing of what Gerald Vizenor calls "hypotragic"[1] representations of history ("A Postmodern Introduction" 11). I will read Highway's trickster within the terms of Vizenor's theories of the potency of humour and transformation in reversing narratives of defeat. An emblem of the stylistic elasticity and parodic mode of Highway's writing, the trickster's shape shifting is also continuous with Mikhail Bakhtin's discussion of the novel as a genre. I will turn to Bakhtin's characterization of this genre as appropriating languages of authority and turning their corresponding socio-ideological systems on their sides. "There takes place within the novel an ideological transvaluation of another's language, and an overcoming of its otherness," Bakhtin notes of this genre (365). These theories will help describe Champion and Dancer's introduction to the residential school and their subsequent struggle to free themselves from its authoritative discourse.

Bakhtin's contrasting views of the novel and poetry propose that the latter is bound by a preoccupation with linguistic and stylistic purity. This description raises productive questions for Rita Joe's poetry about her residential schooling and the effects of this institution on her expression. I will turn to two instances of her poetry, one an elegy and the other a topographical poem, and investigate the congruities between Bakhtin's characterization of poetry and the structure about which Joe writes. What is the relation of form to content in these two poems? What are the silences in these poetic reflections on a place that casts a shadow over the speaker? How does Joe rework the poetic modes she employs?

My investigation of the relation between institutional and discursive containment concludes with a reading of Jane Willis's autobiography, *Geniesh: An Indian Girlhood*. A trenchant examination of her youth spent in the residential school, Willis's narrative centres on her difficult process of reversing its negative impact and shedding her dependence on "'the system'" (26) to regain her self-worth. Although a forceful critique of the values instilled in her by the residential school, *Geniesh* presents a divided and conflicted autobiographical subject. The narrator's estrangement from her family, classmates, and cultural community undermines her emergence at the end of the autobiography as both exemplary and representative of Aboriginal people at large. I will examine the contradictions in this text and treat Willis's use of autobiography as an indication of the extent to which her subjectivity remains tied to the values of the residential school. My investigation will take place on a metatextual level, then, as I argue that Willis's fear of leaving the confines of the residential school corresponds to a similar reluctance to leave the strictures of genre—that is, to write something other than an individually centred autobiography that upholds liberal notions of success and leaves her sense of displacement from her cultural community untroubled.

Note

1 Vizenor's term refers to an overemphasis on tragic themes in the readings of tribal narratives by literary critics and scholars in the social sciences. While this coinage may seem a misnomer, in that "hypo" commonly refers to "lack" or "not enough," this term requires a more intricate interpretation. Chadwick Allen proposes that one read the "hypo" prefix "in terms of 'below, beneath, under' and of 'less than normal, deficient.'" He explains: "For Vizenor's coinage, [...] it is helpful to think of the term 'hypochondria,' which strikes me as the analogy he is drawing from. Hypochondria's literal meaning is 'under the cartilage of the breastbone'; in normal usage, of course, it means 'the persistent neurotic conviction that one is or is likely to become ill.' One way to read Vizenor's term, then, is as a critique of social science and literary theories that operate from the persistent and even neurotic conviction/assumption that all Native stories are or are likely to become tragic." Chadwick Allen, e-mail to the author, 19 May 2004.

FIVE **A Residential School Memoir**

Basil Johnston's
Indian School Days

The publication in 1988 of Basil Johnston's *Indian School Days* initiated an explosion of writing about residential schools in Canada. A narrative re-creation of life at the Garnier Residential School for Boys by one of its "former [...] inmates" (11), Johnston's memoir helped mobilize a collective response to these institutions.[1] Since its publication, a great deal more attention has been directed to the residential school experience, a chapter of Canadian history that extended from the 1870s to the early 1980s. In the same year that Johnston's residential school memoir was published, Celia Haig-Brown's *Resistance and Renewal: Surviving the Indian Residential School* also appeared. A year later, the CBC aired *Where the Spirit Lives*, a film that depicts the devastating effects of an Anglican residential school on an Akainaa (Blood) community in Alberta. Increased media coverage of residential schools followed over the next two years, including an hour-long special by *The Fifth Estate* and commissioned films broadcast on TVO and VisionTV.[2] A number of books on residential schools were published, including survivor accounts such as Isabelle Knockwood's *Out of the Depths* (1992), autobiographies such as Rita Joe's *Song of Rita Joe* (1996) and Tomson Highway's loosely autobiographical novel, *Kiss of the Fur Queen* (1996), as well as a substantial body of critical writing by Aboriginal and non-Aboriginal writers.[3] The traumatic effects of residential schooling came to be known as "residential school syndrome." This belated production of residential accounts produced a secondary effect: skepticism about their effects and actual audience. Do such accounts serve to purge a dominant culture's sense of culpability or to heal a lingering pain in survivors and Aboriginal audiences?[4]

Indian School Days, because of its mild, nostalgic tone, could be considered a text that serves the first purpose—that is, of easing a collective guilt over residential schools. In his review of this book in *Canadian Literature*, Menno Boldt notes with disappointment Johnston's glossing over of the pain of this experience. Boldt criticizes the lack of emotional development in the narrative as well as Johnston's refraining from an explicit indictment of this institution. He also faults the generality with which Johnston depicts the experiences and conflicts in this place. "It seems the author has evaded or repressed the true meaning of his experience," Boldt concludes (312). Boldt's criticisms are interesting, because they unwittingly reveal the type of expectations formed by the wave of media attention described. Jamie S. Scott, on the other hand, finds Johnston's refusal to submit to these preformed judgments to be a strength of this text. Johnston's "delicate balance between justified indignation and considered appreciation for the mixed blessings the school conferred upon its students," Scott maintains, is "a refusal to play upon the guilt-ridden posture" of a liberal readership (151). Reviewer Lisa E. Emmerich joins Scott's appraisal, finding Johnston's "exploration of the relationships forged between students" and the varied, at times sympathetic, relationships formed between the boys and the Jesuits as a "poignant counterpoint to the familiar pairing of well meaning, ethnocentric efforts and the student alienation that policy frequently produced" (219). Johnston, as all of these authors point out, avoids a scriptedness in the way he represents this experience, submitting neither to assumptions of social disintegration nor to a dominant readership's desire for a cathartic narrative.

Johnston's memoir is a much more resistant text than it might appear, not only in its resistance to this type of narrative scriptedness but also in its response to history. *Indian School Days* intervenes in the historical record with an unofficial version of life in a residential school. "None of the stories recounted in this text will be found recorded in any official or unofficial journals of the Garnier Residential School for Boys," Johnston writes in his introduction (11). Francis Hart, in his essay "History Talking to Itself: Public Personality in Recent Memoir" (1979), asserts a similar role for the memoir, distinct from that of institutional history. He describes the memoir as "the personal act of repossessing a public world, historical, institutional, collective" (195). "The memoirs are *of* a person," Hart adds, further characterizing this genre, "but they are 'really' of an event, an era, an institution, a class identity" (195). In her more recent study of the memoir, *Repossessing the World: Reading Memoirs by Contemporary Women*, Helen Buss highlights its value in recording formerly suppressed histories. Her gender-based inquiry emphasizes the appeal of the memoir to those whose experiences and voices have been excluded from official history: "Its concentration on scenes of trauma, initiation, and radical changes in consciousness are performed through the writing, which makes real what the larger culture may not recognize. Set in vivid, scenic recreations of lived experience, the memoir wishes to register as history formerly untold" (23). Like critics before her, Buss places the memoir at the junction of history and autobiography. Narrating in a mode that is both historiographic and idiographic, traversing public and local spheres, the memoir "perform[s] the connections between private lives (ones lived by ordinary people who are not direct actors in large events) and the public ideologies that they are both shaped by and resistant to" (115).

In asserting that the memoir serves writers whose histories have been denied, Buss, however, dismisses the use of the genre by contemporary male writers: "It is women who most often take up the memoir form," she writes, "for the specific purpose of revising their cultural contexts so that their experience is not excluded" (3). "In doing so," Buss continues, these female writers "are bringing female gendering to bear on our previously male-gendered narratives of the self and culture" (3). But Johnston, like the female memoirists Buss describes, also uses this genre to recover a "history formerly untold" (23). His work is an instance of a minority male author's adaptation of this mode, a situation that Buss leaves largely unexamined in her study of gender and genre.

Moreover, Buss argues that the memoir is becoming a predominant mode for female writers because it enables them to explore how their sense of self depends on community. Contemporary women's memoirs unfold around the narrator's negotiation with her defined community to present a subjectivity and narrative that, in Buss's view, are more relational. "In contemporary times, when 'radical individuality' is becoming more a burden than a blessing, new syntheses of group and individual identity factors are being made," she further points out (4). But while Buss acknowledges these "new syntheses of group and individual identity" that are altering the study of life writing, she tends to overlook the memoir's value to male writers such as Johnston, who also wish to articulate a "relational self" (Eakin 43).

Notions about community and self in life writing are linked not only to gender but also to culture. In her essay "First-Person Plural: Subjectivity and Community in Native American Women's Autobiography," Hertha

Sweet Wong examines how the use of the terms "relationality" and "community" in indigenous writing differs from feminist formulations. Wong identifies context as a key factor in determining notions of community, a qualification with obvious relevance to the type of identity formation at work in *Indian School Days*. Within the setting of the residential school, Johnston and his classmates acquire a sense of community that is fraternal and gender-specific. Wong suggests that the invocation of community by Native writers can be a conscious strategy to "resist the official tragic narrative of Indian loss and disappearance" (173). Here Wong's and Buss's studies converge: both emphasize how the articulation of a collective identity can be a way of resisting a silencing, an alienation, or an imposed identity.

Despite its often lighthearted tone, *Indian School Days* contains an undercurrent of resistance—a resistance traceable to the "contrary" version of history it presents. Johnston's extended description of the students' defiance of the priests' authority, his subversion of official discourses, and his affirmation of collective solidarity all serve to articulate a collective identity in opposition to the residential school system. Johnston's collective identity also represents a challenge to the theme of cultural defeat so frequently encountered in conventional narratives of post-contact Native life.

"*Spanish!*"—thus begins Johnston's memoir. "In its most common applications the word refers to a citizen of Spain, and his or her language, and evokes romantic images of señoritas and dons, matadors and conquistadors, flamenco dancers and Don Quixote, castles and courts of inquisition" (1). A word clearly unsuited to the Northern Ontario village bearing the name, its derivation is the subject of local legend. Johnson retells a commonly told tale of a group of Anishnabe warriors who, around 1750, travelled south into Spanish-occupied territory. Enraptured by the Spanish women they encountered on their journey, the warriors took home with them one "winsome señorita," who married an Anishnabe chief, named the village Espanola, and bore descendents bearing the name Espaniol (5).

Johnston casts doubt on the plausibility of this history; even so, it serves an important function at the beginning of his memoir. In a role reversal that runs counter to the process of acculturation so often depicted in colonial chronicles, this inverted conversion tale depicts a European adopting an Anishnabe way of life and the assimilation of a European to an Anishnabe history. For Johnston as for his classmates, "Spanish" evokes yet another, stronger set of associations: "It was a word synonymous with residential school, penitentiary, reformatory, exile, dungeon, whippings, kicks, slaps" (6). "Spanish" becomes a metonymy for the residential schools sustaining the town—St. Peter Claver's Residential School for Indian Boys (later renamed Garnier Residential School) and St. Joseph's Residential School for Indian Girls. Downstream from this village, whose "mixture of French, English, Irish, Scottish, half-breeds, full breeds and one Syrian" all "liv[ed] more or less peacefully with one another" (3), are two reservations whose fishing waters were contaminated by the nearby paper mill, reservations whose "affairs and prospects were governed by an 'Indian agent' who ruled with an autocratic hand and ill-informed dedication," and whose "present [...] was grim, and the future scarcely better" (4). Disturbing the veneer of the otherwise sleepy, peaceful town is the recognition that "what kept the village from extinction [was] 'the school'" (1). The school provided entertainment for Spanish's residents—in the concerts, performances, and sporting events put on by the students—as well as industry for Spanish. The latter fact is made disturbingly evident in Johnston's reminder that the students were under the guardianship of the Minister of Mines and Resources.

These introductory pages of *Indian School Days* cast Johnston in the role of historian, sorting through multiple histories and inserting a new, previously unrecorded account of Spanish. The inverted conversion tale functions as a *petite histoire* or local history of how the village got its name. More important for the historical focus of his text, Johnston brings this local history into dialogue with his classmates' perceptions, for immediately following the playful anecdote is Johnston's more serious commentary on the fear that "Spanish!" evoked in Aboriginal children. The señorita's romantic captivity recedes as Johnston discusses the real incarceration that he and his classmates experienced. A more critical Johnston emerges as the forced confinement of Aboriginal children becomes the focus of his introduction. Alternating between anecdotal and argumentative styles, moving from storyteller to historian, Johnston corrects local accounts of this place with the particular experiences of his classmates.

Johnston's choice of memoir for his residential school account allows this mingling of anecdotal reminiscence and historical revision to continue throughout his text. Using the discursive elasticity of this genre—"a style that is at the same time narrative and essayistic, descriptive and imagistic, factually testimonial and anecdotally fictive" (Buss 2–3)—Johnston depicts the quotidian operations of the residential school both with humour and with incisive criticism. The memoir genre also offers Johnston a flexible perspective. As Marcus Billson points out, the narrator of a memoir moves freely among the rhetorical stances of participant, spectator, and historian (271). Francis Hart further refines this description by referring to the memoirist as a "collective spectator" (204), an observation with particular resonance for *Indian School Days*. "In setting down some of the stories," Johnston writes in the introduction, "I have had to rely on my own memory and on the memories of my colleagues," whose names he proceeds to list (11). In contrast to Menno Boldt's criticism that Johnston's narrative "is frequently interrupted by purposeless listings of names" (311), this acknowledgment anchors Johnston's memoir in the specific and local while also creating a social inclusiveness in his text. More than an expression of authorial gratitude, this statement calls to mind Isabelle Knockwood's collectively inspired residential school narrative *Out of the Depths*. Like Johnston, Knockwood emphasizes the collective significance of her writing and dedicates the book to her peers. Her work goes one step further by creating a context for a collective witnessing that draws on the memories and impressions of her former classmates. Knockwood explains that her motivation for writing the memoir came from other survivors who shared her pain. "I began to feel that I was carrying their pain, as well as my own, around with me," she writes (10). By emphasizing not only the collectivity of this experience but also the collective retrieval of it, *Indian School Days* similarly testifies to a shared, communal history rather than an individual experience of exclusion.

Johnston's acknowledgment of his colleagues' contributions is also a way of authenticating his representation of events. By allowing the perspectives of his classmates to corroborate his own, Johnston outmanoeuvres some of the judgments often levelled at the memoir. "Because of their dependence on narrators who are never fully impartial," Buss notes, "memoirs have been considered to be both bad history (which assumes objectivity) and inferior literature (which prefers narratives that show rather than tell)" (xv). Johnston, however, strives for fairness in his depiction. At the same time, he eschews the expectation, indeed the possibility, of impartiality: "This account of Garnier covering two periods, 1939–44 and 1947–50, is as accurate as memory and affect and bias will allow," he states. "I hope as well that it is fair" (11). As "personal revelation of the event" (Hart 204), memoir makes no claims to objectivity. The memoir attempts to recreate, instead, the texture of daily life in a way that gives history a real, lived dimension.

Memoirs often focus on a segment of the narrator's life, an experience or event that holds wider, historical import: "Titles such as memoirs of *my* times, memoirs *of* San Quentin, memoirs of a girlhood among ghosts, reflect on that ambiguous genitive" (Hart 195). By titling his account *Indian School Days*, Johnston takes the reader to a place and experience that are both generalized and specific. This title also perhaps alludes to *Glengarry School Days* (1902), Ralph Connor's popular turn-of-the-century memoir of a rural Ontario boyhood. *Indian School Days* suggests a similar kind of nostalgic reminiscence, a quality characteristic of the memoir generally.

As Billson observes, "the memoir expresses the memorialist's strong sense of loss for a past which he reveres and misses" (261). Particularly relevant to Johnston's work is Billson's observation that this nostalgic mood prevails "even when that past is one of disappointment and failure" (268). Memoir attempts to recapture "the special, unique, never to be repeated character of the past" (Billson 261). Though this description might seem ill suited to a narrative that revisits an entire youth spent in the residential school, it does capture the fondness with which Johnston looks back on his and his classmates' shared experience. In concentrating on the roguish behaviour of the students—antics that enlivened their daily lives while enabling their psychological survival—Johnston resists the tragic representations of history criticized by Gerald Vizenor and termed by Donald Bahr as "victimist [...] history."[5] Instead, Johnston emphasizes the collective solidarity that he and his classmates formed in this environment, a sense of community that was not broken by the personal and social trauma they experienced.

"Were it not for the spirit of the boys, every day would have passed according to plan and schedule, and there would have been no story," Johnston asserts (47). This statement, presented alongside a schedule of the residents' daily routine, draws attention to what unfolded outside the structure of the residential school's operation. The "spirit" that Johnston attempts to capture is the spirit of resistance, the boys' adeptness at defying the priests. At night in the dormitory, Johnson recalls, there were "muted whispers commingled with muffled giggles" (46). On one occasion, on overhearing the patriotic sentiments of two supervising German prefects, the students exact their own punishment:

> There was always someone awake, someone to hear, someone to whisper aloud, "Nazi"; and the word "Nazi" echoed and re-echoed throughout the dormitory.
> "Who says thees?"
> "Nazi," in the north corner.
> "Who says thees?"
> "Nazi," in the south end.
> "Who says thees?"
> "Nazi." (46)

The German priests, it should be noted, are exiled Nazi sympathizers. "Eventually," Johnston adds, "[Fathers Buck and Kehl] stopped talking to one another in the dormitory and finally learned that it was better to grit their teeth and to bear whatever names the boys called them" (46–47). Because of the anonymous and collective nature of these acts, they are difficult to punish. The narration episodically spotlights these situations where the students use their resources, and quite often their numbers, to challenge the priests' control.

Indian School Days recounts many situations similar to the one above. In showing the irony and quiet transgression behind the boys' conduct and apparent obedience, Johnston also undermines the official discourses of the school. The most pervasive of these institutional discourses is Christian doctrine. When the boys were ordered to "'Kneel down and say your prayers,'" Johnston notes that "we prayed, imploring God to allow us release from Spanish the next day" (45). Johnston recounts with similar skepticism and mockery the boys' tutelage in confession: "Every Thursday night there were confessions to be made, regardless of guilt or innocence" (54). He recalls the boys' organized efforts at avoiding the severe priests: "Of [the four] confessors fathers Richard and Belanger were to be avoided. When the confessors entered the confessional, therefore, the boys quickly formed lines outside the cubicles of the 'easy' priests who, for penance, directed penitents to say 'One Our Father, one Hail Mary and one Glory Be'" (54). On occasions when the stricter priests could not be avoided, the boys neither claimed to be free of sin nor to have sinned too much. "Three was a good number," remembers Johnston, "neither too pious nor too dissolute. 'I fought three times during this past week' was credible and acceptable" (55). What the boys learn from such rituals is not innocence or forgiveness but how to avoid the priests' harangues. "Sinner and innocent alike," Johnston sardonically reflects, "we soon got the hang of confessing" (55).

Outside the confessional, the boys are continually reminded of their inherent guilt. Johnston recalls his lesson in original sin when he and a classmate are mistakenly accused of smoking. His description of the confrontation resembles a criminal interrogation:

> Father looked astounded as I gave my testimony [of innocence] and then, like a lawyer who has caught a witness in a lie during cross-examination, frowned in triumphant indignation, "Oh-ho! So you were smoking, were you?"
> "No, Father."
> "How many puffs?"
> "I wasn' smoking."
> "*Two.* How many puffs?"
> "But I wasn' smoking."
> "*Four.* How many puffs?"
> "I didn' take none."
> "*Eight.* How many puffs?" (160)

Johnston's representation of the exchange in courtroom terms— "testimony," "lawyer," "witness," "cross-examination"—suggests that a criminal-judicial discourse supplemented the Christian one within the school. The questioning continues until Johnston realizes the situation: "At last what Father Hawkins was doing seeped into my skull. He didn't believe me, and he was doubling the number of lashes he was going to deliver on my hands for each untruth that I uttered. I was to be punished for truth instead of being rewarded" (160). "Not wanting sixty-four lashes," Johnston concedes, "I blurted out, 'I took a puff'" (160). The priest responds with the following admonition: "'When are you going to learn to tell the truth? It's one of the lessons that we try to teach you, but if you cannot learn the easy way, then I guess you'll have to learn it the hard way'" (160). These anecdotes call attention to how the disciplinary practices of this institution could run contrary to the principles it purported to instill.

Johnston's critical commentary extends to the political rhetoric justifying the operation of residential schools. He quotes Reverend Wilson, a residential school proponent: "'We don't wish to un-Indianize them, but for their own good induce them to lay aside the bow and fish-spear and put their hand to the plough or make them wield the tool of the mechanic'" (7). These "civilizing" sensibilities justify assimilationist policies: "'We want them to become apprenticed out to white people and to become, in fact, Canadians'" (7). (The economic interests served by this stance are clear: the type of work that Aboriginal people were encouraged to take up was limited to trades and skilled labour jobs.) But "to become [...] Canadian" did not mean straightforward enfranchisement but rather assimilation and indenture. Education was recognized as an important tool of assimilation,[6] an instrument capable of ensuring, in Duncan Campbell Scott's words, that "there is not a single Indian in Canada that has not been absorbed in the body politic" (in Haig-Brown 27). The assimilationist undercurrents of enfranchisement also reverberate in *Out of the Depths*, where Knockwood reproduces school policy: "In the primary grades, instill the qualities of obedience, respect, order, neatness, and cleanliness [...] As the pupils become more advanced, inculcate as near as possible in the order mentioned, independence, self-respect, industry, honesty, thrift, self-maintenance, citizenship and patriotism. Discuss charity, pauperism, Indian and white life, the evils of Indian isolation, enfranchisement" (Knockwood 47–48).

Johnston's position on enfranchisement and assimilation is developed in successive stages of the text. In the introduction he quotes from his valedictory speech, where he appears to extol the value of enfranchisement: "The *Sudbury Star* of June 8, 1950 reported that I had said in my closing remarks as valedictorian: 'Only through having the courage to continue our studies and determination to use the talents we have for advancement can our Indian people become true citizens of Canada'" (12).

The community newspaper, a regional institution representing the dominant culture of Northern Ontario, is eager to depict the "Indian" as already assimilated. Johnston quickly corrects this view: "We were 'wards of the Crown,' not citizens of Canada [...] It was not until 1960 that Indians were allowed to vote in federal elections in Canada" (12). Still, the impression that Johnston leaves here is of the necessity, indeed the desirability, of enfranchisement—the liberal assumption that gaining full citizenship would place Aboriginal people on an equal footing with other Canadians. Near the end of the text, however, Johnston undermines this impression. He returns to his valedictory address once more, prefacing it with the same statement: "It was reported by the *Sudbury Star* that I spoke as follows" (241). Later, to a classmate's question of how he "got all those fancy ideas," Johnston admits that the speech was written not by him but by one of his instructors (241). He loses the speech before addressing the audience, but then describes how he has the good fortune of Father McKenna's text "projecting [...] on my mind's memory screen" (242). This revelation of authorship unsettles the reader's confidence in the statements Johnston spoke on that day. In this closing section of his memoir, Johnston confirms that the possibilities for individual and collective expression within the residential school were few. Even the exemplary valedictorian at the end of his tenure was not trusted to represent himself and his classmates.

On several occasions Johnston questions the suitability and effectiveness of the instruction offered by the residential school: "St. Peter Claver's existed for two reasons. One was to train Indian youth for some vocation [...] Alas, while there were some accomplished farmers and shoemakers, no graduate went into business; the trades for which we had been trained were rendered obsolete by new technology. The school's other purpose was to foster religious vocations by frequent prayer and adoration. But all the prayers, masses, novenas and benedictions could not overcome the natural resistance of most boys to a career in holy orders. The school produced neither tradesmen nor priests" (26–27).

This criticism of education in the residential schools is not uncommon. Lee Maracle writes of her sister "spen[ding] years praying at convent school, cooking delicious pies and ironing the starched paraphernalia of the nunnery and the priesthood along with dozens of other Native girls. She left school at fifteen, functionally illiterate" (38). Isabelle Knockwood makes a similar observation about the male students in her school: "Because so much time was spent in hard physical labour, few of the boys developed more than minimal educational skills" (56). One of Knockwood's former classmates reveals, "'Upon discharge, I was not even able to fill out a job application without help'" (56). Left with this impression of the dubious effectiveness of the residential school, one cannot but read

Johnston's dedication "to all the prefects and priests and teachers who tried to instruct us" as somewhat ironic (11). "Tried to instruct us" rather than "instructed us" is the phrasing Johnston chooses here. The implication is not only that the educational program failed, but also that the attendant political objectives of neutralizing and "absorbing" indigenous subjects into the body politic were not achieved.

Johnston balances his critical commentary on the school with a reminder of the relationships he and his classmates formed in their environment. It is this solidarity, invoked later in life, that occasions the telling of this story. Johnston begins the first chapter by describing a reunion with some of the former residents of the school: "It was an evening of recollection, of reliving the days in Spanish by recalling not the dark and dismal, but the incidents that brought a little cheer and relief to a bleak existence. I share some of these with you" (11). Johnston's affectionate recollection of this time is a way of writing against "aesthetic victimry," in Vizenor's words (in Owens 14). Equally significant is the way in which this assertion of solidarity counters theoretical formulations of the "social dimension of trauma," the view that "trauma damages the texture of community" (Erikson 187). In "Notes on Trauma and Community," Kai Erikson defines collective trauma as a "blow to the basic tissues of social life that damages the bonds attaching people together and impairs the prevailing sense of communality" (187). Erikson further describes the effect of collective trauma on social relationships: "'I' continue to exist, though damaged and maybe even permanently changed. 'You' continue to exist, though distant and hard to relate to. But 'we' no longer exist as a connected pair or as linked cells in a larger communal body" (187). It may be worth pointing out, however, that not all residential school experiences are collectively traumatic in a psychological sense. Johnston affirms the bonds that his community of peers formed within the often denigrating environment of the residential school.

To avoid sounding too celebratory about the social bonds that can form in the midst of trauma, we may keep in mind the numerous other instances in this book where trauma has a negative effect on community. Erikson's description of the social dimension of trauma profoundly recalls the abuse, blame, and dissension within Yvonne Johnson's family.[7] The individual and intergenerational trauma experienced by Johnson's family members results in a fractured group identity. In instances of sexual abuse, moreover, the type of reconciliation we encounter in Johnston's memoir may be far more difficult to achieve. As both *Stolen Life* and *Kiss of the Fur Queen* reveal, this experience has a lasting effect on the individual's subjectivity and ability to identify with others. Markedly absent from *Indian School Days* is any discussion of whether sexual abuse was an experience of the residents. Clearly, Johnston's affirmation of collective solidarity is specific to his individual experiences and perhaps the result of certain representational choices.

Johnston chooses to write against the impression that these institutions created only social disruption and fragmentation within Aboriginal communities. Because subsequent accounts have been much more explicit in their condemnation of the residential school, Johnston's memoir seems perhaps as a milder or more modulated response. But Johnston's narrative remains subversive, not simply because it was one of the first books to deal with the residential schools, but because it uses the memoir as a form of resistance.

While many writers have used memoir to celebrate great acts of history—in CBC parlance, the "heritage moments" that contributed to the making of a Canadian national identity—Johnston returns to a dark and shameful moment in Canadian history. However, he imbues his record of the residential school experience with nostalgia and affection for his fellow students and their capacity to resist this institution's uncontested authority. His complex representation of the residential school is a way of asserting interpretive sovereignty over his experience. Retelling this segment of his life in a way that resists cultural scripts is one of the ways that Johnston recuperates, or "repossesses," his past. Memoir, as Hart describes it, is "the autobiography of survival" (195), of living to tell about "an event, an era, an institution" (195). Johnston's text comes forth with a narrative that, up until its telling, represented an ellipsis in the public's awareness. All of the writings in this book testify to experiences within these carceral structures from the inside. Like the prison texts in the previous chapter, Johnston's writing responds to a type of institutional silencing while also countering the residential school's control and suppression of its occupants. It is fitting, then, that Johnston ends his memoir with a statement by a fellow classmate, whose defiant declaration, "'We toughed it out, didn't we? They couldn't break us down, could they?'" (243) reinforces this text's spirit of collective survival and resistance.

The narrative advantage that the memoir provides Johnston—the opportunity to fashion a public, fraternal identity for himself and to speak, as part of a chorus of voices, against the authority of the institution—is a consideration that follows my discussion of Highway's autobiographical novel, Kiss of the Fur Queen. Like the memoir for Johnston, the novel allows Highway to write about his residential school experience without the level of self-disclosure of an autobiography. The novel also permits an aesthetic distance from the referential grid between the author and the narrator. Fiction can preserve silences in instances where an experience is difficult to claim. It creates an imaginative realm for trauma to be articulated. These representational possibilities combine with the stylistic, discursive, and semiotic play of the novel, elements that Highway uses to write about the official discourses of the school.

Notes

1 I do not mean to suggest that Johnston's was the first narrative account of the residential school. Jane Willis's *Geniesh: An Indian Girlhood* (1973) was an earlier instance of the residential school narrative in Canada. Written in the tradition of the boarding school autobiography, *Geniesh* centres on Willis's youth spent in this institution and its deleterious effects on her life afterward. Willis's text received very little critical attention following its publication and eventually fell out of print. Maria Campbell's *Halfbreed* (1973) and Anthony Apakark Thrasher's *Thrasher: Skid Row Eskimo* (1976) discuss their adolescence in residential schools, but this experience is not the primary focus of either book.

2 Mary Jane Miller documents this surge of media attention in her essay, *"Where the Spirit Lives:* An Influential and Contentious Television Drama about Residential Schools."

3 See, for instance, Agnes Grant, J.R. Miller, Judith Ennamorato, and John S. Milloy.

4 This issue is raised by Roland Chrisjohn and Sherri Young in *The Circle Game: Shadows and Substance in the Indian Residential School in Canada* (1997). Written in reaction to the Royal Commission on Aboriginal Peoples (RCAP), this work intervenes in the "standard account" that emerged from the proceedings on residential schools. Chrisjohn and Young criticize the rhetoric of healing and the pathologizing of "residential school syndrome," which in their view have neutralized discussions of legal recourse and monetary redress.

5 "Just as dichotomized, binary, or Manichean reasoning once served as justification for imperial domination," Arnold Krupat summarizes, "so, too, is it often retained today to justify that form of postcolonial revisionism that produces what Donald Bahr has called 'victimist ... history,' a very specific form of narrative which 'tells how one people was damaged by another'" (316).

6 The 1969 White Paper on Indian Affairs recognized education as a primary tool of assimilation. The National Indian Brotherhood (now the AFN) responded in 1972 with the document "Indian Control of Indian Education" (Monture-Angus 93). Under the Indian Act, enfranchisement was also mandatory for those who received a university education (Tobias 42–48).

7 Erikson's argument also prompts consideration of the effect of the residential school on community formation within Aboriginal cultures. As the discussion in Part One begins to ask, what possible impact did sex-segregated institutions have on the political organization of Aboriginal peoples? I am thinking here of the emergence of groups like the Native Women's Association of Canada and the National Indian Brotherhood. The women interviewed in Janet Silman's *Enough Is Enough: Aboriginal Women Speak Out* further reveal that some of the male-led Native and Métis organizations were unsupportive of Aboriginal women's efforts to have the Indian Act amended so that the status of an indigenous woman would no longer be defined by that of her husband.

six "It is the law"

Disturbing the Authoritative
Word in Tomson Highway's
Kiss of the Fur Queen

In an evocative moment early in Highway's novel, Abraham and Mariesis Okimasis acknowledge their ineffable sadness at their son's encroaching departure for the residential school in the south. "'*Sooni-eye-gimow*'s orders,'" Abraham repeats to himself, a phrase uttered by the local priest, Father Bouchard. Rather than soothe the grief of the two parents, the words reflect their helplessness (40). "*Sooni-eye-gimow*," we learn from the text's gloss, translates literally as "Indian Agent." In a reiteration of this statement's meaning, one that further confirms the finality of the situation, Abraham declares in deference: "'It is the law'" (40).

The addition, "It is the law," creates a distance—here, linguistic, but also ideological—between the speaker and the system enforcing this undesired change. The "semantic finiteness" (Bakhtin 344) of this statement calls to mind Bakhtin's notion of "the authoritative word," a type of discourse fused "with political power, an institution" (343). "Located in a distanced zone," the authoritative word is "the word of the fathers," Bakhtin writes, "a prior discourse" (342). Though authoritative discourse precludes any intervention or play in its transmission, there is potential for its transformation in certain generic contexts. Bakhtin posits the novel as the privileged site where struggle is waged against authoritative discourse. Quite within Bakhtin's formulation of this genre, Highway's novel is a "contact zone" whose "mixing of linguistic forms" signifies a "collision between differing points of view on the world that are embedded in these forms" (360).

Stan Dragland, reviewing Highway's novel, highlights its discursive and aesthetic hybridity, a hybridity that takes after Jeremiah's own "mongrelized life" (Dragland 44). "Page by page," he describes, "it sears through the tragedy of deracination and the casualty-strewn but ultimately triumphant process of cultural revival. But as a whole it holds the competing cultures in suspension and is therefore an *assimilating* text, an exercise of the power to welcome the imperializing culture's art and to ridicule its politics" (44; emphasis in original). In her review of *Kiss of the Fur Queen*, Margery Fee similarly notes Highway's mixing of cultural forms. The innovative work that Highway performs in this discursive and aesthetic blending, Fee claims, "takes Canadian literature in a new direction" (156). Publishing considerations may further reinforce Fee's claim: published by Doubleday Canada, Highway's novel has benefited from wide circulation and a broadly based readership. Like Fee and Dragland, I am interested in the interaction between Cree and non-indigenous expressive forms and frames of meaning in this text. While Fee observes that, in Highway's novel, "salvation comes through the transformative power of music, dance and theatre" (157), I will emphasize the transformations and interventions that take place on the levels of language and narrative.

This examination of *Kiss of the Fur Queen* draws on Bakhtin's theories of the novel to explore Champion and Dancer Okimasis's introduction to the residential school, a place that is, quite literally, a "distanced zone," a realm of the fathers. I will consider the aesthetic dimensions of this traumatic interruption in these two characters' lives. My discussion will then turn to Champion's and Dancer's—or rather, Jeremiah's and Gabriel's—gradual process of "ideological becoming" (Bakhtin 341) and theorize how this process is enacted narratologically. The collision of discrete worlds changes into a multilayered consciousness in Highway's text, a mingling of languages and cultural forms. In the context of contemporary Aboriginal writing, the dissolving of semiotic boundaries can involve, as Catherine Rainwater points out, a subversive entry into the dominant discourse that "exposes the ways in which both Native and non-Native frames of reference constantly undergo revision" (xiv).

Champion and Dancer Okimasis experience a rupture in their worlds when they are hauled away on a plane and taken to Birch Lake Indian Residential School three hundred miles south of their home community of Eemanapiteepitat. This is a place where an alien language is spoken, where their superiors dress in strange vestments, and where both boys are victims of sexual acts difficult to name. Like the narrator in Jane Willis's residential school account *Geniesh*, Champion and Dancer initially build up an excitement about the plane ride that will take them beyond the reaches of their remote community. The aircraft they had seen "swallowing—or, better, spewing out—Josephine, Chugweesees, Chichilia, and other Eemanapiteepitat children" (47) they had also admired hovering in the sky "like dragonflies" (47). Once inside, however, Champion experiences a sinking feeling as he notes that the plane "smelled like gasoline and rubber" and that "the glass in the window felt like plastic: yellowy, scratched, difficult to see through" (47–48). The expectation of finding *K'si mantou* [...] loung[ing] lazily among the clouds as if they were giant fluffed-up pillows" (48) is also disappointed as Champion remarks that "there were no clouds that day, merely an eternal blue" (48).

In the scene that follows this anticlimatic departure, we find Champion in line with other initiates about to have his hair shorn. "Poised for the slaughter" (52), he contemplates an unlikely escape from "the pale blue sheet that held him prisoner" (54). In continuous imagery, the blue sheet restraining Champion recalls the disappointing blue sky of the previous scene as well as the blue robe of the Virgin Mary. When the scissors make their "ruthless sweep" (51) through his wavy hair, he likens the experience to "being skinned alive, in public" (53). The preparatory rituals Champion and the other newcomers experience on their arrival are similar to the rituals recounted in Basil Johnston's and Jane Willis's residential school narratives. In his study of the psychosocial effects of "total institutions"—hybrid establishments that function as both residential communities and formal institutions—sociologist Erving Goffman describes the subject's introduction to such contexts as a systematic "mortification," a stripping of the subject's former means of self-identification (16). Renamed and made virtually indistinguishable from the "hundred bald-headed Indian boys [...] [u]niformly garbed in sky-blue denim shirts and navy denim coveralls" (55), Champion undergoes a sudden, traumatic blow to his identity and world.

Shortly following this institutional "mortification," Champion–Jeremiah—"he was willing to concede that much of a name change, for now" (58)—sits in Catholic catechism class led by the principal, Father LaFleur. Champion–Jeremiah's thoughts as he observes the representations of Christian heaven are remarkably similar to those of young Jimmy in *Inside Out*: "Heaven had a substantial population of beautiful blond men with feathery wings and flowing white dresses, fluttering about and playing musical instruments that Champion-Jeremiah had never seen before" (59). He then notes, "with stinging disappointment, that accordions were nowhere to be seen" (59). An instrument to which he had been early introduced by his father—here a Western cultural object absorbed by indigenous culture—the accordion signifies Champion–Jeremiah's Cree/Métis folk tradition. The accordion is a proxy for his familiar world of Eemanapiteepitat—scenes of the "half-crazed Kookoos Cook" demanding a jig on "the ratty old instrument" (16) as the single-toothed Annie Moostoos dances on. As if to confirm the metonymic relationship between the accordion and Champion's Cree culture, the recognition follows: "Among the people rising from [their] graves to heaven, Champion–Jeremiah tried to spot one Indian person but could not" (59). Heaven is marked by the absence not only of accordions but also of Aboriginal inhabitants.

Where Champion–Jeremiah finds the Indians is in the catechismal hell. Despite Father LaFleur's jolting reminder that "'Hell […] is where you will go if you are bad'" (60), Champion–Jeremiah admits to himself, "Hell looked more engaging" (60). Hell is filled with images more recognizable to him. Its tunnels remind him of "the tunnels he and Gabriel made every winter in the deep snow of Eemanapiteeptitat" (60). The images of "dark-skinned people" "laughing gleefully" and "revel[ling] shamelessly in various fun-looking activities" (60) are equally appealing in their familiarity. Even Father LaFleur's litany of the seven deadly sins Champion–Jeremiah finds titillating. "Lust," the last of the sequence, "burst forth like a succulent, canned plum," he remarks (62). As Champion–Jeremiah carefully inscribes "EVIL" into his scribbler, he cannot help but find "it rather pretty, especially the way the *V* came to such an elegant point at the bottom, like a tiny, fleeting kiss" (62). These passages point to Champion–Jeremiah's reinterpretation of authoritative discourse. As Champion–Jeremiah ponders sacred Christian imagery, he repopulates this realm with images and meanings evocative of a hierarchically lower world. In his exegesis of these concepts, then, he brings this language into the realm of imaginative representation and breaches the distance that holds the authoritative word inviolably intact.

The catechism lesson signifies Jeremiah's introduction to guilt. As he quickly discerns, this is a guilt that is racialized. The residential school also introduces him to sexual acts that despite, or because of, their denial are part of this internalization of guilt. Father LaFleur's own lust drives him to commit sexual acts that are the ultimate violation of the boys' innocence. So strange and fearsome are his nightly visits that Jeremiah, observing them take place, compares the experience to watching "the Weetigo feasting on human flesh" (79). The most reprehensible and fitting correlative he can summon from his frame of reference, the Weetigo signifies the sublimated aspects of this trauma.[1] The Weetigo is Jeremiah's attempt at representing what is, in many ways, unrepresentable. Although a faint recognition tells him that he has witnessed this act before and possibly has been victim to the same violation, he immediately denies this knowledge: "Jeremiah opened his mouth and moved his tongue, but his throat went dry. No sound came except a ringing in his ears. Had this really happened before? Or had it not? But some chamber deep inside his mind slammed permanently shut. It had happened to nobody. He had not seen what he was seeing" (80). The denial that Jeremiah expresses here is the response to a trauma that, on the one hand, exceeds his frame of reference, and on the other, demands its cancellation from the mind of the witness. He intuits that, in this system and in this institution, there are no words for this violation to be called into existence. This experience signifies a "shattering break or cesura in experience" (LaCapra 186) that has a marked effect on everything that follows. The task that Jeremiah and Gabriel face is to integrate the impact of this traumatic break discursively and imaginatively.

When Gabriel and Jeremiah return home to spend a summer with their parents, a potential opportunity arises for them to name these acts in their mother tongue. As their mother, Mariesis, relates a story about a woman who possessed "*machipoowamoowin*," or "bad dream power," Gabriel interprets its relevance to his sexual abuse in the residential school. "'Do '*machipoowamoowin*' mean what Father LaFleur do to the boys at school?'" he asks in English, part in jest, but also in an earnest attempt to give name to his violation. Jeremiah responds to Gabriel's question with a voice "as cold as drops from a melting block of ice" (92). "'Even if we told them,' he warns, 'they would side with Father LaFleur'" (92). The exchange, which takes place entirely in English, escapes Mariesis' comprehension:

> Selecting one of the three Native languages that she knew—English would remain, for life, beyond her reach and that of her husband's—Mariesis turned to Jeremiah. "What are you saying, my sons?"
>
> If moments can be counted as minutes can, or hours or days or years, one thousand of them trickled by before Jeremiah was absolutely sure Gabriel's silence would remain until the day they died. And then he said, his voice flat, "*Maw keegway*." Nothing. (92)

Language, in this instance, preserves their guilt. Gabriel and Jeremiah forfeit the opportunity to name their abuse and attendant shame in Cree. Their denial, "'*Maw keegway*.' Nothing," stems from a lack of confidence in their parents to judge these acts independent of the priest's authority. At the same time, though, Gabriel and Jeremiah's denial might also be a conscious decision to keep this guilt in English, to refuse its entry into the Cree world of their former innocence before the traumatic rupture in their lives.

If Jeremiah and Gabriel maintain their silence in both English and Cree, where then does the liberation of thought and speech from the "authoritative word" occur in this novel? The struggle takes place in a series of metaphors that chart the gradual decline of the dominant discourse, and specifically, of the language of Christianity. The most explicit of these metaphors is the Weetigo, a figure whose signification changes over the course of the novel. The Weetigo moves from evoking a reverential fear—in its association with the priest and the priest's predation of the boys—to becoming a metaphor of the mundane, repugnant swell of modern culture—the mall that "having gorged itself, expels its detritus" (121) and the television that "arrived to devour, digest, and shit out the soul of Eemanapiteepitat" (187). In these increasingly scatological descriptions, the Weetigo is made the subject of mockery, cut down in stature. From its prior connection to the sacred—to the Eucharist and Father LaFleur's dominion over the children—the Weetigo declines into bathos, into a "descent from the sublime to the ridiculous."[2]

This fall is pivotally played out in Jeremiah's retelling of Weesageechak's (the Trickster's) destruction of the Weetigo. Disguised as a weasel, Weesageechak "'crawls up the Weetigo's bumhole'" (118) and "'chew[s] the Weetigo's entrails to smithereens from the inside out'" (120). In its most unvarnished interpretation, this story depicts a triumph over an oppressive force. In a more figural register, the contest between the Weetigo and Weesageechak signifies a struggle between authoritative and demotic discourse. A profanation of the former occurs as the Weetigo's boundaries are violated in the most literal sense. Bakhtin likens this profanation of authoritative discourse to "taboo" (Bakhtin 344). Jeremiah and Gabriel's discussion that follows develops the sociolinguistic implications of this transgression. The word "bumhole," Gabriel tells Jeremiah, "'is a mortal sin in English'" (118). Jeremiah further remarks, "'You could never get away with a story like that in English'" (118). The irony here is that the story, at least as it appears in the novel, is rendered in English. Jeremiah's and Gabriel's framing remarks reinforce the metaphoric meaning of the story: its very translation into English violates the mores of this language. By using English to transmit a story that flouts its rules and boundaries, Jeremiah (or Highway) reoccupies this language and deprives it of its hierarchical status.

Like Weesageechak who destroys this consuming, potent creature from the inside out, this novel does the same to the language of Jeremiah's and Gabriel's own violation—the language of Christianity. The Weetigo moves from evoking an unapproachable awe to being emptied of its authority. The destruction of this creature by Weesageechak is also significant because it supplants the Weetigo, a spectre of the penetrating culture, with the Trickster, who, Highway explains in "A Note on the Text," is "as pivotal and important a figure in our world as Christ is in the realm of

Christian mythology" (n.p.). This novel restores the Trickster to its prior status, countering the belief "that Weesaceechak left this continent when the white man came" (n.p.). Highway's narrative assures us that the Trickster is alive and well, "still here among us—albeit a little the worse for wear and tear" (n.p.).

The Trickster appears throughout the narrative in various guises, and most familiarly in the form of the Fur Queen. A figure that presides over the Okimasis boys' lives like a patron saint, the Fur Queen offers benedictions with her frozen kisses. To his own question, "'Who do you think met Dad. On ... the other side? ... Jesus? Or Weesageechak?'" (298), Gabriel affirms, "'The Trickster, of course, [...] Weesageechak for sure [...] Except, this time, the Trickster representing God as a woman, a goddess in fur'" (298). Gabriel's musings confirm what the reader already knows. The awareness of character and reader converge in this moment as the Trickster's presence is firmly established on both interpretive planes.

Highway's invocation of the Trickster in this novel is part of the undoing of "hypotragedies," to use Vizenor's term once again, an affirmation of resilience and resourcefulness over an ideology of tragedy and defeat. In his essay "The Indian Historical Novel," Alan Velie describes the Trickster as "seal[ing] separations between people and peoples": "The storyteller sends the trickster forth into the world to heal its rifts" (207). In *Kiss of the Fur Queen*, the Trickster applies the balm to the wounds of the characters, but it also embodies the aesthetic and ideological mediation of Highway's narrative. The modelling of a critical enterprise after this figure Vizenor calls "Trickster discourse." "In trickster narratives the listeners and readers imagine their liberation," envisions Vizenor, "and the world is 'deconstructed' in a discourse" ("Trickster Discourse" 194). Vizenor's statement picks up from Charles Russell's view that "social values and systems of order are subject to critical demystification and deconstruction, through which the embattled individual may perceive his or her conceptual freedom" (247). The deconstruction Vizenor envisions is that of dominant discourse and the knowledges it privileges. The reinflection of authoritative discourse can take place on a critical level, then, as indigenous discursive and aesthetic traditions come to interact with European literary forms. This critical transformation confirms Elaine Jahner's assertion that "American Indian writing need not always be the object of critical inquiry; it can also generate critical positions" (178).

Like the adaptable, wayward Trickster, whose playfulness often results in profound changes, the novel genre provides a playful means of upsetting and subverting authoritative discourse. It emerges as a genre capable of reinscribing the discourse of one's subordination. What considerations does *Kiss of the Fur Queen*'s hybrid status as an autobiographical novel raise for life writing? I ask this question as a way of returning to the framing concerns of this study—the serviceability of different genres for authors seeking to write against the institutional discourse authorizing their containment.

Highway's combining of novel and autobiography allows certain advantages that a strict autobiography, for instance, cannot. One of these advantages is the opportunity to transform an unutterable, visceral experience into imaginative representation. Fiction, as E.M. Forster contends, may indeed be "truer than history, because it goes beyond the evidence" (62). That is, fiction can go beyond existing frames of reference that the evidence serves to reify. As Jeremiah learns early on in his time at the school, evidence is an institutionally sanctioned value, just as for many of the prison authors in the second chapter, "truth" is also an official concept whose interpretive parameters exclude certain types of evidence. The Bakhtinian novel is a place where no one has jurisdiction over the truth. In Bakhtin's generic view of the novel, it is specifically the power interests behind different discourses that are revealed in their struggle. Here one's language can emerge from out behind the dominant discourse, renewed and transformed.

A semiotic intervention takes place in *Kiss of the Fur Queen* in which hierarchical and demotic languages intermingle along with their corresponding worlds and systems of meaning. Authoritative discourse—the language of religion and, more broadly, "the law"—is opened up, emptied, and reinfused. Highway's novel privileges a type of play that involves a subversive entry into the dominant discourse, an entry much like Weesageechak's passage into the Weetigo and the disarming of its power from the inside out.

Notes

1 My understanding of the sublime is informed by Dominick LaCapra's discussion of this mode of representation as a response to trauma. "The typical response it evokes is silent awe," he remarks of the sublime (93).
2 This definition comes from Pope's satire, *Peri Bathous, or the art of sinking in poetry* (Drabble 72).

SEVEN Hated Structures and Lost Talk
Making Poetry Bear the Burden

The effect of physical as well as literary structures on expression is the primary focus of my examination of Rita Joe's poetry about her residential schooling. "Hated Structure: Indian Residential School, Shubenacadie, N.S." and "I Lost My Talk" provide poetic reflections on the residential school that, despite their different rhetorical styles, are continuous with each other. These two works appeared in Joe's second book of poetry, *Song of Eskasoni* (1988). Published by the small Charlottetown publishing company, Ragweed Press, and edited by Lee Maracle, *Song of Eskasoni* was the follow-up to Joe's debut, *Poems of Rita Joe* (1978). Rita Joe's statements about her writing convey an ethos of a poet of the people. "The basic reason for my writing and speaking is to bring honour to my people," she writes in her later autobiography, *Song of Rita Joe* (157). Joe also sees herself as a spokesperson or stand-in for indigenous people everywhere. When she was awarded the Order of Canada in 1990, Joe accepted it "on behalf of all the Native people across the world" (Lutz 241).

A songwriter as well as a poet, Joe used the medium of music to reach a wide audience. Her songs show the dual cultural influences on her life and work. "Oka Song" is Joe's response to the Oka crisis; it both justifies Aboriginal resistance and seeks amends between the conflicting sides. "Micmac Honour Song" is a sacred Mi'kmaq prayer sung in chant. "And

Then We Heard a Baby Cry" is a Christian spiritual about the birth of Jesus. Like many Mi'kmaq people, Joe was a practising Catholic. Yet she also privileged traditional indigenous spirituality and held both in esteem. As these varied influences might suggest, Joe desired to bridge the gap between indigenous and non-indigenous worlds. Urging a cross-cultural understanding, she saw her audience as consisting of both Aboriginal and non-Aboriginal people. "Always write positive" was her guiding maxim (Lutz 255). A sense of hope and a desire for reconciliation under-lie Joe's writing.

In her reflections on her residential schooling, Joe insists that she and others who experienced this place must focus on the good, on the value and the instruction these institutions provided. Her discussion of the res-idential school attempts to balance criticism and praise: "I think some of the problems, or a lot of the problems that we see today are really the result of the residential schools. And that must never happen again! [...] But let me tell you about the positive part [...] The positive part was: the people that came from it, the good ones, learned a lot from there. And so many people have gone on, and they have become chiefs, counsellors, and social workers, and they went on to learn!" (in Lutz 257).

In her autobiography, Joe describes telling her husband that they must "forget and forgive" the wrongs that were done (*Song of Rita Joe* 48). This attitude is complicated, however, by the need to confront the negative aspects of her experience in the residential school to give a representa-tion of this place in its entirety. Joe's adage to "forget and forgive" is a point with which David Newhouse, reviewing Joe's autobiography in *Quill & Quire*, takes issue. "We must forgive, but we must not forget" is New-house's response (51). He adds that Joe's writing "will help us not forget" (51). Many of the poems and reflections in *Song of Rita Joe*, as Newhouse adeptly suggests, betray this singular focus on the good. "Hated Structure" and "I Lost My Talk," poems from *Song of Eskasoni* that reappear in her autobiography, disturb such an impression. While Joe seeks to acknowl-edge the positive elements of her residential schooling, her writing also admits the damaging effects of these institutions.

"Hated Structure" uses a topographical poetic form to reflect on this public landmark's personal significance to the speaker. The speaker sur-veys the residential school from a position of physical proximity, strug-gling to maintain a distance between it and herself. Though she achieves a physical and emotional separation from this place, the cadence, voice, and structure of the poem reveal its weight on her expression. This topic is more fully explored in "I Lost My Talk," a poem that addresses the effect of this institution on the speaker's language and identity. In this adaptation of the elegy, the speaker laments not a lost individual or loved one but her "lost talk." In both poems, I will explore the effect of the residential school on the speaker's expression and extend this consideration to poetic concerns. I will probe the spaces for articulation that these two poetic modes offer Rita Joe and trace the possible continuities between the institutional restrictions about which she writes and the restrictions of literary form.

"Hated Structure" opens with a set of directions marking the specific location of Shubenacadie Indian Residential School. "If you are on Highway 104 / In a Shubenacadie town," the speaker addresses the reader, "There is a hill / Where a structure stands" (1–4). Though the poem begins by orienting the reader in relation to this local landscape, the subject of the poem shifts to the speaker in the following two lines, where she describes the response that the structure evokes: "A reminder to many senses / To respond like demented ones" (5–6). This "reminder" applies not to the reader or passing motorist but to the speaker. The speaker's personal response takes over from the reader's perception as she refers to a reaction that, in relation to its surrounding context, is potent. "Demented," or its root, "dementia," suggests the symptomatic responses of memory failure or impaired reasoning ("Dementia"). The use of this word here might imply a denial of an experience that had a traumatic effect on the speaker.

The speaker's observations as she surveys this structure from a closer position point to its ruin. On the floor of this building she once "held in awe" (10) lies a "deluge of misery" (9). She notes "grime everywhere" throughout its interior (13). This place is sullied by its history, haunted by children who "lived in laughter, or abused" (16). The juxtaposition, "lived in laughter, or abused," indicates the different possible interpretations of the children's existence in this structure. On one hand, it implies that their existence consisted of both, the former of which Johnston chooses to emphasize in his memoir. Perhaps laughter was necessary to withstand the abuse, this split description suggests. However, since the line ends with "abused," the poem deflates the impression of this structure as a place of laughter and instead reinforces a bitter perspective of the children's experience there.

The speaker remains on the threshold of this structure, refusing to re-enter it and the memories that exist for her within. She declines the opportunity to walk its floors, wishing not to experience the "fear" they would transmit (20). The interior of this place threatens to overwhelm her with "episodes" she cares "not to recall" (22). But while she consciously refuses to remember, she is, in an oblique and restrained way, re-experiencing these sensations from her point of observation beyond the window. This experience is not as distant as she would like it to be, and the responses that this place evokes in her require a constant and willful act of separation.

In the last five lines of the poem, the speaker manages to achieve her desired distance through literary representation. She muses philosophically:

> The structure stands as if to say:
> I was just a base for theory
> To bend the will of children
> I remind
> Until I fall (23–27)

This removed, objective commentary attempts to neutralize the structure by emptying it of its personal hold over its past occupants. The structure is reduced to a mere "base," without the dimensions of the walls and floors that earlier threaten to enclose the speaker in its space once again. By calling it a structure, and then just a "base for theory," she rids this place of its physical presence. Moreover, Joe's description of it as a "structure" rather than a building or school might allude to the ideological and political structures sustaining the operation of these schools. While the structure stands as a reminder of an unpleasant history, its dominion over the speaker and its survivors will hold only until the building falls. Its calcified, immovable quality permits it to either stand or fall, unlike "the will of children" that can "bend" and adapt. The last line of the poem confirms the structure's final demise. The distance that the speaker creates earlier in the poem by physical separation and by contrasting presentations of past and present culminates in this final image in which the structure collapses in a heap of rubble.

Despite her attempt at channelling attention away from this structure's hold over her, its effect on the speaker manifests itself in her tautness of voice and in the rhythmic unevenness of the composition. The spare description and, at times, shortness of the poetic line contribute to the strained feel of the poem and reveal that the speaker has not quite transcended this structure. The shadow that it casts on the speaker's expression is developed more explicitly in "I Lost My Talk," where the poetic meditation centres on the effect of an imposed language on the speaker's subjectivity.

In "I Lost My Talk," the speaker mourns the loss of her language, her former means of cultural identity. The "you" she addresses in the poem represents the historical, colonizing force responsible for seizing this language from her. "I speak like you / I think like you," she declares, and even more interestingly for the focus of this chapter, "I create like you / The scrambled ballad, about my word" (6–9). These lines create a self-reflexive dimension to the poem that prompts us to read the poetic creation as something alien to the speaker, an imposed form that limits her full expression. Preceded by the definite article "the" rather than the possessive "my," the "scrambled ballad" is a removed object, something that does not quite fit her "word." The syntactic disjointedness of this line reinforces the "scrambled" feel of her expression.

On the one hand the word "scrambled" means unintelligible, confused. Yet, it may also imply hybridity, a combination of elements. The speaker confirms this impression as she opens: "Two ways I talk" (10). She continues to suggest the capacity of this "scrambled" language to articulate her view: "Both ways I say" (11). "Your way is more powerful," she states unequivocally (12). In this statement is an awareness of the hierarchical difference of the two voices she has acquired. The poem ends optimistically, however, as the speaker entreats her listener: "Let me find my talk / So I can teach you about me" (14–15). These lines hold the promise of cultural knowledge extending two ways rather than one.

This poem explores the effects of an imposed language on the speaker's expression, a struggle that extends to poetic form. As the speaker reveals, this received language affects her type of creation. Halfway into the poem, however, she shifts from lamenting the loss of her mother tongue to asserting that her talk still exists within this imposed language. "Two ways I talk," the speaker declares, "Both ways I say" (10–11). Her former language is a means of self-representation waiting to be recovered. Thus, while this poem initially points to the restrictions of poetic form—the "ballad" that does not fit her word—it concludes by identifying the potential for the speaker to make this form her own. The liberating power of this reinflection calls to mind Louis Owens's exhortation: "Rather than merely reflecting back [...] the master's own voice, we can, in an oft-quoted phrase, learn to make it bear the burden of our own experience" (xiii).

"I Lost My Talk" and "Hated Structure" are both reinscriptions of Western poetic modes. In "I Lost My Talk," Rita Joe turns to the elegy to mourn a specific cultural loss that is the result of an institutionalized colonization. Its concluding lines instill the hope of reconciliation through intercultural negotiation, a type of mediation not unlike that in *Kiss of the Fur Queen*, where different aesthetics, languages, and belief systems meet and interact with each other. "Hated Structure" similarly adapts a well-established poetic mode to a place and experience that belie its traditional application. This inversion is signalled by the poem's opening, where the speaker, rather than surveying the structure from an elevated position in the convention of the topographical poem, is dwarfed by the school that looms above her from its placement atop a hill.[1] The school's elevation dissolves over the course of the poem until its final fall at the end. In her inscription of this mode, Rita Joe emphasizes this structure's ruin rather than its former glory, while also musing over its significance in a painful rather than nostalgic or lauding manner. Joe's writing, by her own description, wages a "gentle war" against dominant representations of Aboriginal history and life (in Steele 12).

My reading of Jane Willis's autobiography, *Geniesh*, pushes the connection between physical and discursive containment by investigating the restrictions of genre that an author may not be able to transcend. While Willis brings to her autobiography an experience of the residential school survival that was largely unarticulated at the time of her writing, her handling of genre reflects a reluctance to make this form fully her own. This "rise above the challenges" story emphasizes Willis's self-made success, a success that she contrasts with the helpless passivity of her cultural community. I will concentrate on the autobiographical identity Willis fashions for herself within the narrative and demonstrate how this identity continues to uphold the values and prejudices instilled in her by the residential school.

Note

1 Margaret Drabble further describes this poetic mode: "Many topographical poems are also 'prospect poems,' i.e. written from a high point, surveying a large view, and many were written in praise of particular parks, estates, and gardens, evidently in the hope of patronage" (989–90). This mode saw a resurgence in the late twentieth century, with an emphasis on country scenes and on a vanishing rural culture (Drabble 990).

EIGHT

Autobiography as Containment
Jane Willis's *Geniesh:
An Indian Girlhood*

Published in 1973, the same year as Métis author Maria Campbell's *Halfbreed*—an autobiography that would become a seminal text in Aboriginal-Canadian literature—*Geniesh: An Indian Girlhood* spans Willis's childhood, from on a remote island in James Bay to her ten-and-a-half years at residential schools in Fort George, Quebec, and Sault Ste. Marie, Ontario. Her narrative combines the naive and humorous reflections of a young "Geniesh"—an adored and indulged child of an extended family—with her sad and bitter coming of age in residential schools. In these institutions she is taught to renounce her shameful, dirty, and savage inheritance. Writing in the vein of boarding school autobiography—a tradition that reaches back to the American "Carlisle Success Story" and the "civilizing" fervour to "Kill the Indian, Save the Man!"—Willis plays back the prejudices that she was led to internalize in the process of showing "what Indians can accomplish" (Willis 132).

"Kill the Indian, Save the Man" was the motto of the Carlisle Indian School's founder, General Richard Henry Pratt. Touted as "the Father of Indian Education," Pratt opened the first Carlisle school in Pennsylvania in 1879 (Brumble 138). Twenty-four more schools opened in the United States over the next twenty years (Bensen 9). The boarding school narrative emerged from campaigning efforts to convince parents to send their children to these "away schools." Fictionalized propaganda by non-indigenous writers, as well as autobiographies by former students, were published and circulated throughout indigenous communities.

The very title of Willis's work invites comparison with earlier indigenous life-narratives such as Zitkala-Sa's (Yankton Sioux) *Impressions of an Indian Girlhood* (1900), Charles Eastman's (Santee Sioux) *Indian Boyhood* (1902), and Luther Standing Bear's (Oglala Sioux) *My Indian Boyhood* (1931). Willis's narrative moves from an idyllic childhood in the remote, natural environment of her home community to her acculturation in the "civilizing" institution of the residential school to a final stage in which she regains her sense of personal integrity. Eastman, who went on to receive a medical degree following his Carlisle schooling, describes his education as a process in which "I had most of my savage gentleness and native refinement knocked out of me" (in Murray 79).[1] In similar strain, Willis looks back on her residential schooling as an attempt "to educate the *savage* out of us" (120; italics in original). As David Murray remarks of Eastman's autobiography,[2] the narrative is double-voiced, affirming his success in the white world while also critiquing the "civilizing" institutions that brought about the rupture in his personal and cultural identity. Similar tensions, I want to propose, run through Willis's text. Underlying this autobiography is an experience of alienation and disidentification, an autobiographical subject who defines herself by her difference from others. The book's contradictory impulse to raise up Willis's story as representative of an entire culture and at the same time to assert her difference, her disconnection from her cultural origins, results in an uncertain text.

It is primarily in the figuration of the autobiographical subject, a subject set apart from her family and social matrix by her desire for upward mobility, that Willis seems to remain within the rigid parameters of traditional Western autobiography. Even though her story relates to a larger, historical struggle of Native people to maintain their cultural sovereignty in the face of regulatory institutions such as the residential school, this autobiography is individualized in focus. The narrator views herself as distinct from her family and community from the beginning of the narrative. Her first mark of difference is that she is born of a White father, whom her mother refuses to marry because of the church's scorn for mixed marriages. Geniesh, or Janie, is raised by her grandparents when her mother later marries an Aboriginal man from another village. Janie's mixed blood separates her from her maternal family, who regard her less desirable traits as the outcome of miscegenation: "It was my white-tainted blood that made me so stubborn, so curious, so pesky, so contrary—all the traits a good, obedient, and pliant little Indian was not supposed to have. I had heard people say it often enough" (10–11). As a child, she sensitively observes her treatment by her relations and begins to identify herself as different from them. This distance that emerges early in the narrative foretells the later separation she will undergo from her family and community.

Janie's first rejection of her family occurs when she desires to leave the security and warmth of her grandparents' home to attend the Anglican residential school on the island. She initially perceives St. Philip's Indian and Eskimo Anglican Residential School as a place of privilege. Her preference for the Anglican, and not the Catholic, school is the result of prejudicial shaping: "The missionaries had done their job well and I was terrified of Catholics. I did not want to live in some dumb old Catholic school; I wanted to live at 'The St. Philip's Indian and Eskimo Anglican Residential School of Fort George, Quebec, Canada'" (27). The two schools on the island serve different pockets of indigenous communities. The Catholic school is "othered," as are its students, who are mustered from the "other Indian settlements on both sides of the bay" (26). Janie remarks that only the students from marginal territory attend the Catholic boarding school, a detail that further conveys the Anglican Church's purchase over the community. These prejudiced attitudes, inculcated by missionary influence, form a perceptual screen through which Janie beholds her ideals during the early part of her life.

Janie's pleas to attend the residential school are finally placated, and she is admitted to the school on a day basis. Despite its inauspicious welcome, she remains eager for the opportunity to become a resident of the school rather than reside with her grandparents: "I looked forward to August [...] when I too would become one of the privileged, living, not just attending classes, at the school" (36). Admittedly, this is the voice of a young narrator whose desire to attend the school is, in part, the desire for inclusion, to be part of the community of her peers. At the same time, however, these musings reveal her early internalization of the privilege associated with White institutions. Once Janie enters the school as a full-time resident, her anticipation and expectations are soon disappointed. She undergoes the ritual of having her hair shorn and deloused with kerosene, being renamed, and receiving a "compartment number" to contain her personal effects. Still, she reveals a sense of pride in her newly acquired identity: "Though I reeked of kerosene, Lifebuoy soap, and mothballs, and probably looked like a refugee, I felt like a model. I made sure my shoes were in plain view so everyone could admire them. The fact that all the girls received identical clothes made no difference to me. I felt that I alone stood out from all the rest"(40). Janie clings to her sense of individuality as she is reduced in appearance to those around her. Failing to heed the warnings of her classmates about the terrible treatment that awaits her at the school, she reflects, "I thought it would be different for me. After all, I was the sun, and the most important figure in the Universe; all life revolved around me" (42). The self that Willis presents here is fiercely individualistic, insistent on its own centrality. She later admits, "The most difficult adjustment I had had to make upon entering the boarding school had been accepting the fact that I was no longer the important person I had been at home—or liked to believe I was anyway. I was just one of the crowd of little savages who had to be saved" (74). Beneath the irony, Willis reveals that the school eroded the one thing she valued most—her individuality.

The residential school operates much like a prison: in its endeavour of acculturating the girls, it breaks them into subservience and self-abasement. As Linda Warley points out, repeated reference to the school as "prison-like" equate this structure with Foucault's concept of a "carceral space," a place of regulation and surveillance. Janie recognizes the extent of this control when she is denied the opportunity to attend her grandfather's funeral. She mourns not only her grandfather's passing, but also her loss of agency: "The blinding tears flowed freely as I mourned the loss of my beloved grandfather and realized yet another loss, something I could not yet put into words, something intangible—the freedom to be a human being" (81). Restricted from making any decisions over her life during her time there, Janie experiences a loss of freedom that is both crippling and dehumanizing. She later looks back on "the suffocating, dehumanizing, prison-like atmosphere of the school" (186)—an impression that is disjunctive with her earlier eagerness to attend this institution. "The school I had entered with such great expectations," she admits without prevarication, "had turned out to be a prison" (121).

In an interesting inversion, however, the prison comes to represent safety. The school is promoted to its residents as a protective haven from the corruption that awaits the girls outside. Paradoxically, the school offers protection from the corrupting White world, even though this institution is operated by White people. The outside world thus figures as an absence/presence in the residential school, where what is prohibited is continually invoked. After listening to the radio series *Dragnet* while cleaning the Reverend's house, Janie assumes this distorted perspective of the outside world: "I turned on the radio and listened to the monotone, spine-tingling voice of Jack Webb on *Dragnet* confirm the dire warnings of the ministers, and I wondered why I wanted to leave my island sanctuary and risk my precious life by going out into that raping, murdering, plundering world outside" (110). In a Foucauldian mechanism, the students regulate their own imprisonment, become the agents of their surveillance. When

Janie graduates from St. Philip's, she is reluctant to leave her carceral space. Later, at the Shingwauk Indian Residential School in Sault Ste. Marie, a teenage Janie admits, "I welcomed the chance to stay close to the security of the school, prison-like as it was" (153). What is a reprehensible, insufferable place throughout Janie's time there ultimately renders her immobile, afraid to move beyond its confines.

The residential school succeeds in cleaving a distance between Janie and her family. When she returns to her community after graduation, she feels her difference even more acutely than before. Her changed perspective is no more evident than in her reaction to her mother's living quarters: "I walked in expectedly, but I was appalled at the shabbiness and seediness that surrounded me. Had I, for fifteen years, lived amid such utter poverty? Had I become a snob—as my friends had predicted I would—looking down at my own people and their old ways? My outlook and my feelings, I told myself, could not have changed so drastically in a few years" (172). Despite her insistence to the contrary, Janie has acquired a class consciousness. She asks herself repeatedly, "'How can they live like that?'" (173). She no longer feels close to her family and resents her mother's pleas for her to stay on the island: "I could not explain to her that as much as I loved the people and the way of life, I still felt that something was missing from my life. People like her and my grandmother, with very little or no education, were totally content with the simple life. They did not feel the urge to change or to explore other ways. I envied them their naiveté and their happiness. Education had robbed me of this inner peace and contentment" (122).

Janie's time in the system causes her to disidentify with her family. She is displaced from her traditional culture and ill equipped to accept the role her family assumes of her. She views her return to the island as an interruption to her process of development. It is in urban society—"the safety of the vast, impersonal world outside"—that she feels most "free" (185). Her process of regaining a sense of place, however, leaves her belonging neither to her traditional community nor to dominant White culture, whose ideology and institutions she appears unable to forgive.

Despite her difficult and at times problematic admissions, Willis carries out a steady critique of the prejudices that took a great part of her early life to shed. Part of the focus of this autobiography—its indictment of the institutions that left countless Native children in this country "believing that 'Indian' was synonymous with 'sub-human,' 'savage,' 'idiot,' and 'worthless'" (199)—affirms its status as a defiant text. In terms of the content of this text, its sharp indictment of dominant society's disregard for the autonomy and cultural integrity of First Nations groups, Willis's autobiographical act represents, in Sidonie Smith and Julia Watson's choice of phrase, an "articulation through interrogation" ("De/Colonization" xx). A counter-narrative to the ideologies forced upon Willis in the residential school, *Geniesh* contests the institution responsible for her subjugation and wrests back her sense of personal integrity through the medium of autobiography.

Yet, frequently in *Geniesh*, the narrator's self-descriptions approximate how others see her. The skewing of inward and outward perception in this text reveals the extent to which Willis's subjectivity is defined by the dominant values of her institutional context. One of the more salient features of this text is the narrator's combined internalization and subversion of stereotypes pertaining to Aboriginal people. Colonial constructions figure throughout the narrative as the narrator turns these perceptions onto herself. Janie, in effect, rises into Aboriginal stereotypes. She deploys these stereotypes in an often ironic way, yet there is also a measure of identification in them. Overwhelmed at the strangeness of her first English class, Janie describes feeling "like a dumb old Indian" (34). This perception carries over to the end of her autobiography, where she indignantly distinguishes herself from "the majority of Indians" in her home community, who remain "like children," helplessly dependent on the government for their direction and livelihood (198). The flipside to the values by which she distinguishes herself is their embedded prejudices, prejudices she redirects back at her cultural community.

This combined adherence to and subversion of the dominant values of her institutional context characterizes Janie's behaviour toward the residential school staff. When one of the teachers identifies her as Janie Esquinimau rather than Janie Matthews on her first day at school, she defers to the teacher's authority: "'If she wants to call me Janie Esquinimau,' I thought, 'that is her right. After all, she is white'" (32). A little further into the narrative, Janie remarks of the same teacher: "By the end of the long, exhausting day, I saw her as a god-like, super-human being" (34). This God-like status carries over to White people generally: "We also believed that white people [...] were superior beings. We had been brought up to look upon them as gods [...] Our belief in the superiority of the white race grew stronger as we grew older" (49). The reverence that Janie admits here, even when counterpointed with instances where she undermines the staff's competence, contributes to this autobiography's divided stance toward institutional authority. Janie only subtly explains the reasons for her submission later in the narrative, when she fails to comprehend an allusive remark made to her by an Indian Agent: "I did not know what he meant but I grinned and nodded," she describes. "It was always best to agree with a white man, even if he did not make sense" (133).

Linda Warley notes a similar economy of capitulation and subversion in Willis's text. As Warley points out, the narrator of *Geniesh* overturns cultural stereotypes but also internalizes many of the constructions she attempts to resist. Warley concludes by conceding that Willis does not—or cannot—entirely extricate herself from the discourse available to her within the space of an autobiography: "Although Native life writing can be understood as an act of political agency, in that the Native writer represents her experiences [...] from her own perspective, the extent to which the Native autobiographer writing in English can distance herself from the discursive structures that have represented her as a 'dirty savage' is necessarily limited" (85). These statements connect Willis's unfirm handling of colonial authority with the restricted potential for representation that autobiography offers. Willis's expression of her subjectivity is limited: she cannot fully inscribe herself within the discourse and genre available to her at the time of writing. The publication date of Willis's autobiography should be seen as key to some of the tensions that emerge in our subsequent reading of this work. However, while Maria Campbell's autobiography made a significant impact on its readership—indigenous and non-indigenous alike—and continues to be recognized as a watershed work in an Aboriginal literary canon, *Geniesh* fell into oblivion. The bitterness and alienation that Willis reveals as she affirms her individual success story indicate that her success comes at a cost—at the cost of her identification with her family and home community, whom she claims to represent at the end of her autobiography. While she eventually leaves the residential school, its impact on her sense of self continues to be seen in the narrative.

On further examination of this text, the divide between Willis and her family becomes more noticeable. The dedication of this book reads: "*To my mother, whose lack of faith made this story possible, and to my husband, whose faith made this book possible*" (n.p.; italics in original). In the final pages of her autobiography, Willis openly condemns her family's racial prejudice toward her husband, who is White. The tone of this epilogue differs noticeably from the rest of the narrative. She likens her relationship with her family to her debilitating reliance on government support: "My dependency on Indian Affairs was broken overnight, but my dependency on my family took longer to sever. The years of forced separation had only served to strengthen my emotional ties to them, too much so" (198). Willis' withdrawal from her family is achieved with her marriage to her husband: "My first step towards breaking that dependency was taken when I married Bud. My family, though having nothing against him other than his race, disapproved of my choice for a husband. I am certain that what annoyed them more was the fact that I had managed to find a wonderful man without any help from them whatsoever" (198). Willis's assertion of independence involves a reinvestment of her identity through her husband. It is critical to remember that at the time of Willis's writing she would have lost her "Indian status" by marrying a White man. In a similar irony, her so-called "enfranchisement" under the Indian Act would have brought about a change of legal status and perhaps a change in her own sense of identity.[3]

Although she neglects to address this fact in her narrative, Willis's independence by enfranchisement is at the sacrifice of her cultural identity and the very tribal rights that secure it. In a somewhat darker parallel to *Stolen Life*, the individual success Willis celebrates in her autobiography is at the expense of her relationship with her family. Janie's privileging of dominant institutions early in the narrative never entirely recedes in this work. While she recognizes her loss of freedom on her entry to the school and asserts a quiet resistance to her treatment within it, she develops a security in this institution that, in the end, renders her afraid to leave it. By the end of her autobiography she is emotionally and geographically removed from her family. On the back flap of the book, fittingly appearing at the end of the narrative, is a picture of a smiling Jane Willis with this caption: "Jane Willis now lives in Hollywood, California with her husband William [Bud] and four children. She returns to Fort George on James Bay in Quebec for several months every second summer." This description of Willis's migration curiously suggests her ties to her family that she elsewhere abjures. At the same time, this extratextual signage reinforces Willis's individual passage. Willis's residency in Hollywood, the quintessential terminus of prosperity and material attainment, emblematizes her worldly expansion beyond her remote origins.

While the issues this work takes on suggest a resistant stance, Willis measures herself by many of the restrictive prejudices she purports to shed. Although this text unravels and contests the ideologies manifest in the operation of the residential school, Willis's handling of autobiography keeps a number of these values intact in the trajectory of success it carves. Could this work, as Linda Warley argues, express a complex dialectical struggle with the limited subjectivity of Western autobiography? Or does Willis, offered the choice of reinscribing this tradition, ultimately abstain, reluctant to leave the confines of this genre? Is there a third space somewhere between these choices that recognizes Willis's complex and subtle resistance in taking up a genre that, at the time of her writing, was inhospitable to an indigenous female subjectivity—a literary form so rife with ideological significance that her entry would, alone, represent an act of resistance?

The reasoning to which this text leads us is that in different social contexts, liberalism and its attendant genres like autobiography can allow for social critique, even if such a critique does not fall on the values and ideological history of the genre itself. The perception that Willis's autobiography fails to be transgressive enough is, in some ways, an unfair judgment, informed by recent developments and perspectives of this genre. My consideration of Willis's handling of autobiography, then, needs to be qualified by a recognition that the desires and expectations imposed on a text can be contained by their own critical moment and specific history. Still, in Willis' autobiography there is a blind spot that neglects to recognize how, in the process of proving "what Indians can accomplish," Willis maintains some of the very prejudices she claims to reject and measures her success against the apparent incompetence and passivity of her people.

Although Willis does not entirely manage to write against the language of her confinement, her struggle is continuous with that of the other authors in this part of this book. Rita Joe addresses the relation between institutional and discursive restriction more explicitly; and perhaps because of her recognition of the residential school's effect on her subjectivity, she comes closer than Willis to transcending this structure. Highway uses the spaces of fiction and the novel to overturn the language of his subordination. While its presence in Highway's text is slight, the residential school comes to affect not only the individual lives of his characters but also, in my estimation, his aesthetic choices. The impact of institutional context on an author's selection of a certain genre is more direct in *Indian School Days*, where Johnston uses the memoir to assert the collective solidarity of his classmates, to undermine the priests' authority and the ideologies undergirding the school's operation, and to intervene in the public record of this place. Like the authors in the first part of this book, these writers speak out against their physical and discursive confinement while undermining the value and public identity of these institutions. Each text can develop our awareness of the extent to which subjectivity is a function of discourse. Carceral writing is a nearly allegorical mode for such a function, for seizing within writing the potential to liberate oneself and one's history through the act of self-representation. This act applies generally to these authors' responses to a central institution in First Nations history. In Rita Joe's words: "The brave part is in taking on history and leaving your own story" (*Song of Rita Joe* 170).

Notes

1 This passage is from Eastman's second autobiography, *From the Deep Woods to Civilisation* (1916), published fourteen years after *Indian Boyhood*.

2 Murray is speaking here about Eastman's *From the Deep Woods to Civilisation*.

3 Under the *Indian Act*, a Status Indian woman who married a non-Status man lost her Indian status. Along with it, she lost her band membership, which included "her property, inheritance, residency, burial, medical, educational and voting rights on the reserve" (Silman 12). This "legislated sexual discrimination" was repealed in 1985, four years after the United Nations ruled in favour of Sandra Lovelace's case and found Canada in breach of an International Covenant of Civil and Political Rights. For the personal accounts of the Tobique women's collective mobilization against this legislation, see Janet Silman's *Enough Is Enough: Aboriginal Women Speak Out*.

Conclusion

The question posed at the beginning of this study of what carceral writing is leads us to consider, rather, what this literature does. Its performative function is more distinct than that of literature in general. It is socially engaged art, but its engagement is at least partly involuntary—it cannot help but be shaped by the conditions and exigencies of its creation. The writing of a convicted author often serves as a second hearing—one that rebuts representations by legal, judicial, and penal institutions and makes a plea to a wider audience. For authors writing about their residential schooling, their works serve as important rebuttals to the historical record. Both bodies of literature offer a valuable window onto how social contexts affect the use of form. Often pushing the conventions of genre, these authors call attention to the representational capacities of the literary forms they engage.

The incarcerated authors in Part One draw on conventions of prison writing such as the confession, the apology, or the metaphor of the afterlife. Many of them, however, go beyond the traditional applications of the genres they employ. Leonard Peltier describes the prison as an unearthly space, but the conversion experience depicted in his work substitutes an Anishnabe-Lakota cosmology for a Christian one. Yvonne Johnson, too, turns to discursive forms familiar to prison writing such as confession and apology, yet her telling spills into other genres to articulate the full weight of her story. These writers demonstrate through their writing their non-neutral position before the law, before a non-Aboriginal readership, and even in relation to the political ideologies embedded in the genres they take up. All diverse examples of life writing, these works show how incarcerated Aboriginal writers use the autobiographical act as a means to resist an identity conferred on them by the legal-judicial system.

Similar expansions of form emerge in writings about the residential school featured in Part Two of this book. The authors appearing in these chapters take existing forms and modes such as the memoir, the elegy, and the topographical poem—genres that have a distinct cultural tradition—and reinflect them with their unique experiences. In "I Lost My Talk" Rita Joe envisions the potential to represent herself through an imposed language and received literary forms. Emblematic of other residential school writing examined in this section, Joe's poem self-reflexively ponders the author's ability to make the form her own. The writing featured in both Part One and Part Two invites consideration of how the use of form can be a personal as well as a political act.

A number of the works featured in this examination have had a significant impact on public dialogues outside of their immediate publication contexts. The proliferation of residential school accounts in the 1990s played a crucial role in adjusting public perceptions of these institutions. So numerous became these accounts that they drew the question as to whether a normative telling was beginning to emerge. Basil Johnston's representation of his time at "Spanish" provides a corrective to the scripted narrative that Roland Chrisjohn and Sherri Young, for instance, criticize in their discussion of the Royal Commission on Aboriginal Peoples (RCAP) hearings. Other residential school accounts, such as those of Rita Joe and Isabelle Knockwood, have provided a context for a collective healing and affirmation. These works join the outpouring of testimony in other global contexts. As Gillian Whitlock points out in her examination of Stolen Generation testimony in Australia, the recent emergence of truth and reconciliation commissions in Australia, Canada, and South Africa has provided an outlet for working through colonial legacies and for sending out calls for reform. While shaped by global politics, these testimonies have taken different local expressions, Whitlock points out, and have opened up important intercultural dialogue. Signifying an alternative public hearing, residential school works like the ones highlighted in this book have provided an impetus for a broader national community to confront the more blighted parts of Canadian history.

Some of the writing in this book has led to interventions in the legal-judicial system. Following the publication of *Stolen Life*, the Assembly of First

Nations petitioned the federal Minister of Justice for Yvonne Johnson's case to be reviewed.[1] These developments point to the afterlife of texts—that is, to their engagement with legislative structures, judicial institutions, and public perceptions in ways that exceed the act of reading. It can be argued that Stolen Life's reaching of a wide market audience has helped alter the public's view of the criminal justice system and whom it punishes.

Accompanying these shifting public attitudes have been concrete changes in the legal system: Aboriginal communities are gaining greater control over the administration of justice, and the courts are increasingly recognizing the legitimacy of indigenous beliefs in their proceedings and rulings. In a remarkable example, a judge presiding over a murder case on Manitoulin Island acquitted the accused, Anishnabe Leon Jacko, for clubbing to death another Anishnabe man, Ron Thompson. The murder was ruled an act of self-defence motivated by the accused's belief that the victim was a Bearwalker. In its coverage of the court case, the right-wing magazine *Alberta Report* paraphrased Basil Johnston on the function of Bearwalkers in Anishnabe culture: "Bearwalkers [...] are hired by tribesmen too weak to attack a personal enemy on their own. The Ojibway sorcerers reputedly can transform themselves into any sort of animal to get near their intended victim and implant a noxious substance in that person's body, causing severe illness and even death" (Sillars 22). In his acquittal of the accused, Judge Trainor concluded: "'I accept the evidence of native spirituality as being a sincerely held belief'" (Sillars 22). These instances point to the transformations that are taking place in Canadian jurisprudence now that it is beginning to acknowledge indigenous world views. Texts like the ones in this book have played no small role in this transformation.

In considering indigenous peoples' relationship to institutions of justice and state policy, this book has emphasized the cross-currents between the experiences of indigenous people in Canada and the United States. This bifurcated awareness dispels any notion that Canada has a kinder relationship with those Aboriginal peoples residing within its borders. Indeed, Canada failed as a protective haven for Yvonne Johnson and Leonard Peltier. Both initially saw Canada as an asylum. Johnson escaped from Butte, Montana, after being let off on a manslaughter charge. "'I had dealt with official law,'" she explains to Wiebe. "'But in Butte there's cop law too, and that one really counts'" (143). "'But ... you got away?'" Wiebe asks Johnson as they continue to discuss this point in her life. "And suddenly," he narrates, "she grins at me, her quick, luminous smile. 'Canada'" (144). Later, Johnson reflects on the inverted fate of her forebear: "A hundred years ago Big Bear's son, Little Bear, escaped from the Canadian prairies to hide in the mountains of Montana; I was born and raised all over those mountains; now I was running back to hide north of the border" (152).

Johnson's flight north bears some interesting resemblances to that of Peltier, who, after the acquittal of the two other suspects in the FBI murders, slipped across the border. He was arrested by the RCMP, confined to a Vancouver jail, and extradited on the basis of what were later contested as false affidavits. Canada offered Johnson temporary respite from her desperate circumstances in Montana, yet it was not long before she was pulled into the seedy culture of Winnipeg's skid row, where most of her relatives were living. In Wetaskiwin, Johnson ended up among questionable companions, who involved her in a murder. Johnson's trajectory was not the same as Peltier's experience of organized state conspiracy, but in each instance, Canada disappointed their expectations as a sanctuary from desperate circumstances in the United States. For Johnson and Peltier, Canada became an invisible and then a real prison, a continuation of the confinement and lack of agency they encountered south of the border.

At many points while writing this work, I have been poignantly reminded that I am dealing not just with texts but with lives. On learning of James Tyman's fate after writing his autobiography or hearing about Yvonne Johnson's transfer from Okimaw Ohci Healing Lodge, I realized perhaps more than ever before the limitations of literary criticism and the contingencies of the readings we construct from texts. Many of these narratives continued after the publication of the writing, making the "conclusions" drawn in literary discussion not only limited but in many ways ethically questionable. Still, literary criticism has an important role to play in providing this literature with an audience, an audience these authors may have been denied in the past by the law, by limited access to publishing institutions, or by social prejudice. "Intrinsic to the study of this literature," Michael Hogan observes of prison writing, "is the dialogue it attempts to engage us in. It is a literature of confrontation: direct, naked, desperately committed. There can be no passive reader, no indifferent listener" (96).

Indeed, these texts often extend what we consider to be "literature," by adapting literary forms and using writing as a vehicle for a social message. This writing as a whole also asks us to evaluate our place in relation to it and to contemplate our acts of reception. Can we approach these works solely for purposes of consumption, aesthetic interest, or academic dissection, or does this writing ask different things of us? An outcome of this study has been that recognition that these texts ultimately demand our engagement on a social, not just a literary or interpretive, level.

Note

1 This information was posted on the Assembly of First Nations' website 23 July 1999. www.afn.ca/resolutions/1999/aga%20resolutions%201999/res74.htm.

Works Cited

Adams, Howard. *Prison of Grass: Canada From the Native Point of View*. Toronto: New Press, 1975.

Allen, Chadwick. "Blood as Narrative / Narrative as Blood: Declaring a Fourth World." *Narrative* 6, no. 3 (1998): 236–55.

———. "Re: Vizenor Question." E-mail to the author, May 19, 2004.

Anderson, Kim. *A Recognition of Being: Reconstructing Native Womanhood*. Toronto: Second Story, 2000.

Antone, Elaine. "I lay in my prison cell all night long." *Tribal Ways* 74 (1974): n.p.

Arias, Arturo. "After the Rigoberta Menchú Controversy: Lessons Learned about the Nature of Subalternity and the Specifics of the Indigenous Subject." *MLN* 117, no. 2 (2002): 481–505.

———, ed. *The Rigoberta Menchú Controversy*. Minneapolis: University of Minnesota Press, 2001.

Assembly of First Nations. "Yvonne Johnson Support." July 23, 1999. www.afn.ca/resolutions/1999/aga%20resolutions%201999/res74.htm.

Bahr, Donald. "Indians and Missions: Homage to and Debate with Robert Costo and Jeannette Henry." *Journal of the Southwest* 31 (1989): 300–29.

Bakhtin, Mikhail. *The Dialogic Imagination: Four Essays*, ed. Michael Holquist, trans. Caryl Emerson and Michael Holquist. Austin: University of Texas Press, 1981.

Batisse, Ken George, et al. *Native Sons*. Cobalt: Highway Book Shop, 1977.

Bauman, Richard. *Verbal Art as Performance*. Prospect Heights, IL: Waveland, 1984.

Beard, Laura J. "Giving Voice: Autobiographical/Testimonial Literature by First Nations Women of British Columbia." *SAIL* 12, no. 3 (2000): 64–83.

Bensen, Robert, ed. *Children of the Dragonfly: Native American Voices on Child Custody and Education*. Tucson: University of Arizona Press, 2001.

Berg, Paul. Letter to the President of the United States. *Leonard Peltier Defense Committee*. hartford-hwp.com/archives/41/367.html.

Beverley, John. "The Margin at the Center: On *Testimonio* (Testimonial Narrative)." In Smith and Watson, *De/Colonizing the Subject*. 91–114.

Billson, Marcus. "The Memoir: New Perspectives on a Forgotten Genre." *Genre: Forms of Discourse and Culture* 10 (1977): 259–82.

Bird, Gloria. "Breaking the Silence: Writing as 'Witness.'" In *Speaking for the Generations: Native Writers on Writing*, ed. Simon J. Ortiz. Tucson: University of Arizona Press, 1998. 26–48.

Bliss, Karen. "Robbie Robertson Sets Sights High on New Album." *Canoe— Jam! Showbiz*. January 27, 1998. jam.canoe.ca/Music/Artists/R/Robertson_ Robbie/1998/01/27/749308.html.

Blue. "For Strong Women." *Tightwire* (1991): 11.

Boldt, Menno. "Residential School." Review of *Indian School Days*, by Basil Johnston. *Canadian Literature* 124–25 (1990): 311–12.

Breytenbach, Breyten. *True Confessions of an Albino Terrorist*. London: Faber and Faber, 1984.

Brown, Dee. *Bury My Heart at Wounded Knee: An Indian History of the American West*. New York: Holt, Rinehart and Winston, 1971.

Bruchac, Joseph. "Breaking Out with the Pen: Poetry in American Prisons." In Harris and Aguero, eds., *A Gift of Tongues*. 286–94.

———. "The Decline and Fall of Prison Literature: Funding and Market Factors Stifle Inmate Voices." *Small Press* (January–February 1987): 28–32.

Brumble, David. *American Indian Autobiography*. Berkeley: University of California Press, 1988.

Buss, Helen. *Repossessing the World: Reading Memoirs by Contemporary Women*. Waterloo: Wilfrid Laurier University Press, 2002.

Campbell, Maria. *Halfbreed*. Toronto: McClelland and Stewart, 1973.

Camus, Albert. *The Myth of Sisyphus and Other Essays*. Trans. Justin O'Brien. New York: Vintage, 1991.

Canada. Office of the Correctional Investigator. *Annual Report of the Office of the Correctional Investigator of Canada 2005–2006*. September 2006. www.oci-bec.gc.ca/reports/AR200506_e.asp#AboriginalOffenders.

———. Parliament. Senate Standing Committee on Legal and Constitutional Affairs. *Proceedings*, no. 14, February 12, 1998. 36th Parliament, 1st Session. www.parl.gc.ca/36/1/parlbus/commbus/senate/com-e/lega-e/14ev-e .htm?Language=E&Parl=36&Ses=1&comm_id=11>.

Cardinal, Harold. *The Unjust Society*. Edmonton: Hurtig, 1969.

Cariou, Warren. "The Racialized Subject in James Tyman's *Inside Out*." *Canadian Literature* 167 (2000): 68–84.

Cartoon [no title]. *Tightwire*. 1976. 41.

Caruth, Cathy. *Unclaimed Experience*. Baltimore: Johns Hopkins University Press, 1996.

Cassil, C. "The Raven." *Words from Inside* 5 (1976): 6–7.

Chrisjohn, Roland, and Sherri Young, with Michael Maraun. *The Circle Game: Shadows and Substance in the Indian Residential School Experience in Canada*. Penticton, BC: Theytus, 1997.

Clifford, James. "On Ethnographic Allegory." In *Writing Culture: The Poetics and Politics of Ethnography*, ed. James Clifford and George Marcus. Berkeley: University of California Press, 1986. 98–121.

Connor, Ralph. *Glengarry School Days: A Story of Early Days in Glengarry*. Toronto: Westminster, 1902.

Cooper, Ronald. Introduction. In Batisse, *Native Sons*. n.p.

Couser, G. Thomas. "Making, Taking, and Faking Lives: The Ethics of Collaborative Life Writing." *Style* 32, no. 2 (1998): 334–50.

Cruikshank, Julie, with Angela Sidney, Kitty Smith, and Annie Ned. *Life Lived Like a Story: Life Stories of Three Yukon Native Elders*. Vancouver: UBC Press, 1990.

Culleton, Beatrice. *In Search of April Raintree*. Winnipeg: Pemmican, 1983.

Davies, Ioan. *Writers in Prison*. Toronto: Between the Lines, 1990.

"Dementia." *Oxford English Dictionary*, 2nd ed. 1989.

Dickason, Olive Patricia. *Canada's First Nations: A History of Founding Peoples from Earliest Times*. Toronto: McClelland and Stewart, 1992.

Dimock, Wai Chee. *Residues of Justice: Literature, Law, Philosophy*. Berkeley: University of California Press, 1996.

Dorris, Michael. *Paper Trail: Essays*. New York: HarperCollins, 1994.

Drabble, Margaret, ed. "Bathos." *Oxford Companion to English Literature*, 5th ed. Oxford: Oxford University Press, 1985. 72.

———. "Topographical Poetry." *Oxford Companion to English Literature*, 5th ed. Oxford: Oxford University Press, 1985. 989–90.

Dragland, Stan. "One Story, Many Stories." Review of *Kiss of the Fur Queen*, by Tomson Highway. *Canadian Forum*, October 1998: 44–46.

Eakin, Paul John. *How Our Lives Become Stories: Making Selves*. Ithaca, NY: Cornell University Press, 1999.

Eastman, Charles. *From the Deep Woods to Civilisation* [1916]. Lincoln: University of Nebraska Press, 1977.

Egan, Susanna. "Telling Trauma: Generic Dissonance in the Production of *Stolen Life*." *Canadian Literature* 167 (2000): 10–29.

Emmerich, Lisa E. Review of *Indian School Days*, by Basil Johnston. *Western Historical Quarterly* 22 (1991): 219–20.

Ennamorato, Judith. *Sing the Brave Song*. Schomberg: Raven, 1998.

Erikson, Kai. "Notes on Trauma and Community." In *Trauma: Explorations in Memory*, ed. Cathy Caruth. Baltimore: Johns Hopkins University Press, 1995. 183–99.

Fast, Robin Riley. "'It Is Ours to Know': Simon J. Ortiz's *From Sand Creek*." *SAIL* 12, no. 3 (2000): 52–63.

Fee, Margery. "Perfect Cree." Review of *Kiss of the Fur Queen*, by Tomson Highway. *Canadian Literature* 176 (2003): 156–57.

———. "Writing Orality: Interpreting Literature in English by Aboriginal Writers in North America, Australia, and New Zealand." *Journal of Intercultural Studies* 18, no. 1 (1997): 23–39.

Felman, Shoshana. "Education and Crisis, or the Vicissitudes of Teaching." In Felman and Laub, eds., *Testimony*. 1–56.

———, and Dori Laub, eds. *Testimony: Crises of Witnessing in Literature, Psychoanalaysis, and History*. New York: Routledge, 1992.

Felski, Rita. "On Confession." In Smith and Watson, eds., *Women, Autobiography, Theory*. 82–95.

Forster, E.M. *Aspects of the Novel*. 1927. London: Edward Arnold, 1953.

Foucault, Michel. *Discipline and Punish: The Birth of the Prison*. Trans. Alan Sheridan. New York: Vintage, 1995.

Franklin, H. Bruce. *Prison Literature in America: The Victim as Criminal and Artist*. Rev. ed. New York: Oxford University Press, 1989.

Friedberg, Lilian. "Dare to Compare: Americanizing the Holocaust." *American Indian Quarterly* 24, no. 3 (2000): 353–80.

Gaucher, Robert. "The Canadian Penal Press: A Documentation and Analysis." *Journal of Prisoners on Prisons* 2, no. 1 (1989): 3–24.

———. "Inside Looking Out: Writers in Prison." *Writing as Resistance: The Journal of Prisoners on Prisons Anthology (1988–2002)*, ed. Robert Gaucher. Toronto: Canadian Scholars' Press, 2002. 33–49.

Gilmore, Leigh. *The Limits of Autobiography: Trauma and Testimony*. Ithaca, NY: Cornell University Press, 2001.

Glaremin, T.A. "The Four Seasons of Prison." *Tightwire*, Summer 1993: 16.

Goffman, Erving. *Asylums: Essays on the Social Situation of Mental Patients and Other Inmates*. New York: Anchor, 1961.

Graburn, Nelson H.H. "The Fourth World and Fourth World Art." In *In the Shadow of the Sun: Perspectives on Contemporary Native Art*, ed. Gerhard Hoffmann. Quebec: Canadian Museum of Civilization. 1–26.

Grant, Agnes. *No End of Grief: Indian Residential Schools in Canada*. Winnipeg: Pemmican, 1996.

Gready, Paul. "Autobiography and the 'Power of Writing': Political Prison Writing in the Apartheid Era." *Journal of South African Studies* 19, no. 3 (1993): 489–523.

Guiney, Frank. "Poetry in Prison." *Words from Inside* 2 (1972): 3–7.

Haig-Brown, Celia. *Resistance and Renewal: Surviving the Indian Residential School*. Vancouver: Tillacum, 1988.

Hall, Anthony. *The American Empire and the Fourth World,* vol. 1. Montreal: McGill-Queen's University Press, 2003.

Harlow, Barbara. *Barred: Women, Writing, and Political Detention.* Middletown, CT: Wesleyan University Press, 1992.

———. *Resistance Literature.* New York: Methuen, 1987.

Harris, Marie, and Kathleen Aguero, eds. *A Gift of Tongues: Critical Challenges in Contemporary American Poetry.* Athens: University of Georgia Press, 1987.

Harris, Michael. *Justice Denied: The Law versus Donald Marshall.* Toronto: Macmillan, 1986.

Hart, Francis. "History Talking to Itself: Public Personality in Recent Memoir." *New Literary History* 11, no. 1 (1979): 193–210.

Henke, Suzette. *Shattered Subjects: Trauma and Testimony in Women's Life-Writing.* New York: St. Martin's Press, 1998.

Highway, Tomson. *Kiss of the Fur Queen.* Toronto: Doubleday, 1998.

Hileman, Sharon. "'Yes, I Can': Empowerment and Voice in Women's Prison Narratives." In *No Small World: Visions and Revisions of World Literature,* ed. Michael Thomas Carroll. Urbana, IL: National Council of Teachers in English, 1996. 58–71.

Hogan, Michael. "Some Further Observations on the Convict as Artist." *New Letters* 47, no. 1 (1980): 83–96.

Jahner, Elaine. "Metalanguages." In Vizenor, ed., *Narrative Chance.* 155–85.

JanMohamed, Abdul, and David Lloyd. "Toward a Theory of Minority Discourse: What Is to Be Done?" In *The Nature and Context of Minority Discourse.* Oxford: Oxford University Press, 1990. 1–16.

Joe, Rita. "And Then We Heard a Baby Cry." *Song of Rita Joe: Autobiography of a Mi'kmaq Poet.* Charlottetown: Ragweed, 1996. 182–83.

———. "Hated Structure: Indian Residential School, Shubenacadie, N.S." *Song of Eskasoni: More Poems of Rita Joe.* Charlottetown: Ragweed, 1988. 75.

———. "I Lost My Talk." *Song of Eskasoni: More Poems of Rita Joe.* Charlottetown: Ragweed, 1988. 32.

———. "Justice." *Lnu and Indians We're Called.* Charlottetown: Ragweed, 1991. 55.

———. "Lament of Donald Marshall, Jr." *Song of Eskasoni: More Poems of Rita Joe.* Charlottetown: Ragweed, 1988. 70.

———. "Oka Song." *Song of Rita Joe: Autobiography of a Mi'kmaq Poet.* Charlottetown: Ragweed, 1996. 174–75.

———. "Micmac Honour Song." *Song of Rita Joe: Autobiography of a Mi'kmaq Poet.* Charlottetown: Ragweed, 1996. 184–85.

———. *Song of Rita Joe: Autobiography of a Mi'kmaq Poet.* Charlottetown: Ragweed, 1996.

Johnston, Basil. *Indian School Days.* Norman: University of Oklahoma Press, 1988.

Johnston, Patrick. *Native Children and the Child Welfare System*. Toronto: Canadian Council on Social Development and James Lorimer, 1983.

Kadar, Marlene. "Coming to Terms: Life Writing—from Genre to Critical Practice." In *Essays on Life Writing: From Genre to Critical Practice*, ed. Marlene Kadar. Toronto: University of Toronto Press, 1992. 3–16.

Kalman, Judy. "A Bakhtinian Perspective on Learning to Read and Write Late in Life." In *Bakhtinian Perspectives on Language, Literacy, and Learning*, ed. Arnetha F. Ball and Sarah Warshauer Freedman. Cambridge: Cambridge University Press, 2004.

Kaplan, Caren. "Resisting Autobiography: Out-Law Genres and Transnational Feminist Subjects." In Smith and Watson, *De/Colonizing the Subject*. 115–38.

Keeshig-Tobias, Lenore. "Let's Be Our Own Tricksters, Eh." *Magazine to Reestablish the Trickster: New Native Writing* 1, no 1 (1988): 2–3.

———. "Stop Stealing Native Stories." *Globe and Mail*, January 26, 1990, A7.

King, Thomas. "Godzilla vs. Post-Colonial." *World Literature Written in English* 30, no. 2 (1990): 10–16.

Knockwood, Isabelle, with Gillian Thomas. *Out of the Depths: The Experiences of Mi'kmaw Children at the Indian Residential School at Shubenacadie, Nova Scotia*. Lockeport, NS: Roseway, 1992.

Kroeber, Karl. "Technology and Tribal Narrative." In Vizenor, ed., *Narrative Chance*. 17–37.

Krupat, Arnold. *Ethnocriticism: Ethnography, History, Literature*. Berkeley: University of California Press, 1992.

LaCapra, Dominick. *Writing History, Writing Trauma*. Baltimore: Johns Hopkins University Press, 2001.

LaRocque, Emma. "Here Are Our Voices—Who Will Hear?" In *Writing the Circle*, ed. Jeanne Perreault and Sylvia Vance. Norman: University of Oklahoma Press, 1993. xv–xxx.

Laub, Dori. "An Event Without a Witness: Truth, Testimony, and Survival." In Felman and Laub, eds., *Testimony*. 75–92.

Lejeune, Philippe. *On Autobiography*, ed. Paul John Eakin, trans. Katherine Leary. Minneapolis: University of Minnesota Press, 1989.

"The Loon and the Blind Man." In Batisse et al., *Native Sons*. 54–55.

Lutz, Hartmut, ed. *Contemporary Challenges: Conversations with Canadian Native Authors*. Saskatoon: Fifth House, 1991.

MacLennan, Hugh. Introduction. In *The Time Gatherers: Writings from Prison*, ed. Gertrude Katz. Montreal: Harvest House, 1970. 1–5.

Mannette, Joy. *Elusive Justice: Beyond the Marshall Inquiry*. Halifax: Fernwood, 1992.

———. "The Social Construction of Ethnic Containment: The Royal Commission on the Donald Marshall Jr. Prosecution." In Mannette, *Elusive Justice*. 63–77.

Manuel, George, and Michael Posluns. *The Fourth World: An Indian Reality*. Don Mills, ON: Collier-Macmillan, 1974.

Maracle, Lee. *Sojourner's Truth and Other Stories*. Vancouver: Press Gang, 1990.

Marowits, Ross. "Ontario Reintroduces Legislation to Stop Criminals from Profiting from Crime." Canadian Press. June 5, 2001.

McFarlane, Peter. *Brotherhood to Nationhood: George Manuel and the Making of the Modern Indian Movement*. Toronto: Between the Lines, 1993.

McLeod, Neal. "Coming Home Through Stories." In Ruffo, ed., *(Ad)dressing Our Words*. 17–36.

McMaster, Gregory. "Maximum Ink." *Journal of Prisoners on Prisons* 10 (1999): 46–52.

Menchú, Rigoberta. *I, Rigoberta Menchú: An Indian Woman in Guatemala*, ed. Elisabeth Burgos-Debray, trans. Ann Wright. London: Verso, 1984.

Miller, D. Quentin. "'On the Outside Looking In': White Readers of Nonwhite Prison Narratives." In Miller, ed., *Prose and Cons*. 15–32.

———, ed. *Prose and Cons: Essays on Prison Literature in the United States*. Jefferson, NC: McFarland, 2005.

Miller, J.R. *Shingwauk's Vision: A History of Native Residential Schools*. Toronto: University of Toronto Press, 1996.

Miller, Mary J. *"Where the Spirit Lives*: An Influential and Contentious Television Drama about Residential Schools." *American Review of Canadian Studies* 31, nos. 1/2 (2001): 71–84.

Milloy, John S. *A National Crime: The Canadian Government and the Residential School System, 1879–1986*. Winnipeg: University of Manitoba Press, 1999.

Momaday, N. Scott. *House Made of Dawn*. New York: Harper and Row, 1968.

Monture-Angus, Patricia. *Thunder in My Soul: A Mohawk Woman Speaks*. Halifax: Fernwood, 1995.

Ms. Cree. "Entrenched Social Catastrophe." *Journal of Prisoners on Prisons* 5, no. 2 (1994): 45–47.

Murray, David. *Forked Tongues: Speech, Writing, and Representation in North American Indian Texts*. London: Pinter, 1991.

Native Council of Canada. *Métis and Non-Status Indian Crime and Justice Commission. Report of Métis and Non-Status Indian Crime and Justice Commission*. 1977.

Neve, Lisa, and Kim Pate. "Challenging the Criminalization of Women Who Resist." In *Global Lockdown: Race, Gender, and the Prison Industrial Complex*, ed. Julia Sudbury. New York: Routledge, 2005. 19–33.

Newhouse, David. Review of *Song of Rita Joe: Autobiography of a Mi'kmaq Poet*, by Rita Joe. *Quill & Quire*, July 1996: 51.

Nobis, Ray, Jr. "Ballad of Ron Cooper." In Batisse et al. *Native Sons*. 52–53.

Olney, James. *Autobiography: Essays Theoretical and Critical*. Princeton: Princeton University Press, 1972.

Owens, Louis. *Mixedblood Messages: Literature, Film, Family, Place*. Norman: University of Oklahoma Press, 1998.

Paul, Marianne. *When Words Are Bars: A Guide to Literacy Programming in Correctional Institutions*. Kitchener, ON: Core Literacy, 1991.

Peltier, Leonard. *Prison Writings: My Life Is My Sun Dance*. New York: St. Martin's Press, 1999.

Petrone, Penny. *First People, First Voices*. Toronto: University of Toronto Press, 1983.

———. *Native Literature in Canada: From the Oral Tradition to the Present*. Toronto: Oxford University Press, 1990.

Prohibiting Profiting from Recounting Crimes Act of 2002. www.e-laws .gov.on.ca/html/statutes/english/elaws_statutes_02p02_e.htm.

Rainwater, Catherine. *Dreams of Fiery Stars: The Transformations of Native American Fiction*. Philadelphia: University of Pennsylvania Press, 1999.

Rarihokwats. Foreword. In Solomon, *Eating Bitterness*. n.p.

Reid, Bill, and Robert Bringhurst. *The Raven Steals the Light*. Vancouver: Douglas and McIntyre, 1984.

Ross, Luana. *Inventing the Savage: The Social Construction of Native American Criminality*. Austin: University of Texas Press, 1998.

Ross, Rupert. *Returning to the Teachings: Explaining Aboriginal Justice*. Toronto: Penguin, 1996.

Rousseau, Jean-Jacques. *Confessions* [1781]. Trans. Angela Scholar. Oxford: Oxford University Press, 2000.

Royal Commission on the Donald Marshall, Jr., Prosecution. Halifax: Government of Nova Scotia, 1989.

Ruffo, Armand Garnet, ed. *(Ad)dressing Our Words: Aboriginal Perspectives on Aboriginal Literatures*. Penticton: Theytus, 2001.

Russell, Charles. *Poets, Prophets, and Revolutionaries: The Literary Avant-Garde from Rimbaud Through Postmodern*. New York: Oxford University Press, 1985.

Salter, Liora. "Science, Advocacy, and the Media." Unpublished paper presented at the conference "Commissions of Inquiry: Lawyers' Values and Public Policy Makers' Values," Dalhousie Law School, February 1988.

Sands, Kathleen Mullen, and Theodore Rios. *Telling a Good One: The Process of a Native American Collaborative Autobiography*. Lincoln: University of Nebraska Press, 2000.

Scheffler, Judith A. "Imprisoned Mothers and Sisters: Dealing with Loss Through Writing and Solidarity." In Miller, ed., *Prose and Cons*. 111–28.

———. *Wall Tappings: An International Anthology of Women's Prison Writings 200 to the Present*, 2nd ed. New York: Feminist Press, 2002.

Scott, Jamie S. "Colonial, Neo-Colonial, Post-Colonial: Images of Christian Missions in Hiram A. Cody's *The Frontiersman*, Rudy Wiebe's *First and Vital Candle*, and Basil Johnston's *Indian School Days*." *Journal of Canadian Studies* 32, no. 3 (1997): 140–61.

Sillars, Les. "Not Guilty by Reason of Native Religion: An Ojibway Indian Is Acquittted for Clubbing to Death a Demon Named Ron Thompson (Leon Jacko Case)." *Alberta Report*, June 16, 1997.

Silman, Janet. *Enough Is Enough: Aboriginal Women Speak Out*. Toronto: Women's Press, 1987.

Sinobert, Al. "The Long and Bitter Trail." Editor's Note. *Tribal Ways* 74 (1974): n.p.

Smith, Sidonie, and Julia Watson, eds. *De/Colonizing the Subject: The Politics of Gender in Women's Autobiographical Practices*. Minneapolis: University of Minnesota Press, 1992.

———. "De/Colonization and the Politics of Discourse in Women's Autobiographical Practices." In *De/Colonizing the Subject*, xiii–xxxi.

———. *Women, Autobiography, Theory: A Reader*. Madison: University of Wisconsin Press, 1998.

Solomon, Arthur. *Eating Bitterness: A Vision Beyond the Prison Walls*, ed. Cathleen Kneen and Michael Posluns. Toronto: NC Press, 1994.

———. "The Wheels of Injustice." *Tightwire*, Spring 1991: 36.

Spender, Stephen. "Confessions and Autobiography." In Olney, *Autobiography*. 115–22.

Standing Bear, Luther. *My Indian Boyhood*. New York: Houghton Mifflin, 1931.

Statistics Canada. "Juristat: Adult Correctional Services in Canada, 2004/2005." October 2006. www.statcan.ca/english/freepub/85–002-XIE/85–002-XIE 2006005.pdf.

Steele, Charlotte Musial. "Rita Joe Wages Gentle War of Words." *Atlantic Advocate*, January 1991: 11–13.

Stoll, David. *Rigoberta Menchú and the Story of All Poor Guatemalans*. Boulder, CO: Westview, 1998.

Street, Brian. *Literacy in Theory and Practice*. Cambridge: Cambridge University Press, 1984.

Sugar, Fran, and Lana Fox, comp. "Survey of Federally Sentenced Aboriginal Women in the Community." Ottawa: Task Force on Federally Sentenced Women, 1990.

Sugars, Cynthia. "Settler Fantasies, Postcolonial Guilt: The Compromised Postcolonialism of Jane Urquhart's *Away*." *Australian Canadian Studies* 19, no. 2 (2001): 101–18.

Swann, Brian. Introduction. In *Harper's Anthology of Twentieth Century Native American Poetry*, ed. Duane Niatum. San Francisco: Harper and Row, 1988. xiii–xxxii.

Taylor, Douglas. "Prison Slang and the Poetics of Imprisonment." In Miller, *Prose and Cons*. 233–45.

"Testimony." Def. 5 a. and 5 b. *Oxford English Dictionary*, 2nd ed. 1989.

Thrasher, Anthony Apakark. *Thrasher: Skid Row Eskimo*. Toronto: Griffin, 1976.

Thomas, Elizabeth. Address to the Canadian Association of Elizabeth Fry Societies, Ottawa, October 3, 2002.

Tobias, John. "Protection, Civilization, Assimilation: An Outline History of Canada's Indian Policy." In *As Long as the Sun Shines and Water Flows: A Reader in Canadian Native Studies*, ed. Ian Getty and Antoine Lussier. Vancouver: UBC Press, 1983. 39–55.

Turner, Dale. *This Is Not a Peace Pipe: Towards a Critical Indigenous Philosophy.* Toronto: University of Toronto Press, 2006.

Turpel, M.E. "Further Travails of Canada's Human Rights Record: The Marshall Case." In Mannette, *Elusive Justice.* 79–101.

Tyman, James. *Inside Out: An Autobiography by a Native Canadian.* Saskatoon: Fifth House, 1989.

Velie, Alan. "The Indian Historical Novel." In *Native-American Writers,* ed. Harold Bloom. Philadelphia: Chelsea Books, 1988. 195–209.

Vizenor, Gerald, ed. *Narrative Chance: Postmodern Discourse in Native American Indian Literature.* Albuquerque: University of New Mexico Press, 1989.

———. "A Postmodern Introduction." In Vizenor, ed., *Narrative Chance.* 3–16.

———. "Trickster Discourse." In Vizenor, ed., *Narrative Chance.* 187–211.

Warley, Linda. "Unbecoming a 'Dirty Savage': Jane Willis's *Geniesh: An Indian Girlhood.*" *Canadian Literature* 156 (1998): 83–103.

Weiss, Gail. *Body Images: Embodiment as Intercorporeality.* New York: Routledge, 1999.

Whitlock, Gillian. "In the Second Person: Narrative Transactions in Stolen Generations Testimony." *Biography* 24, no. 1 (2001): 197–214.

Wiebe, Rudy. *The Temptations of Big Bear.* Toronto: McClelland and Stewart, 1973.

———, and Yvonne Johnson. *Stolen Life: The Journey of a Cree Woman,* 2nd ed. Toronto: Vintage, 1999.

Willis, Jane. *Geniesh: An Indian Girlhood.* Toronto: New Press, 1973.

Witherup, Bill. Preface. In *Words from the House of the Dead: Prison Writings from Soledad,* ed. Bill Witherup and Joseph Bruchac. Trumansburg, NY: Crossing, 1974. n.p.

Wong, Hertha D. Sweet. "First-Person Plural: Subjectivity and Community in Native American Women's Autobiography." In Smith and Watson, eds., *Women, Autobiography, Theory.* 168–78.

Young-Ing, Greg. "Aboriginal Text in Context." In Ruffo, ed., *(Ad)dressing Our Words.* 233–42.

York, Geoffrey. *The Dispossessed: Life and Death in Native Canada.* Toronto: Lester and Orpen Dennys, 1989.

Yúdice, George. "*Testimonio* and Postmodernism." *Latin American Perspectives* 18, no. 3 (1991): 15–31.

Zitkala-Sa. *Impressions of an Indian Girlhood* [1900]. In *Online Archive of Nineteenth-Century U.S. Women's Writings,* ed. Glynis Carr. Winter 1999. www.facstaff.bucknell.edu/gcarr/19CUSWW/ZS/IIC.html.

Index

A

Aboriginal peoples: and carceral continuum, 3–5, 11–12; colonization/dispossession of, 2–3, 7–8, 9, 40, 51, 74–75; criminalization/guilt of, 2–8, 9–10, 11, 34–35, 55; and enfranchisement/assimilation, 96–97, 100n6; non-Aboriginal authors on, 52–53; in representations of heaven, 42, 103–104; and state/judicial policy, in Canada and U.S., 16–17, 30, 127–28

Aboriginal prison writing, 1–16, 23–28, 125–26; as "alternative hearing," 13–14, 31, 65, 125; and ballad, 73–74, 79–80; and colonization/dispossession, 2–3, 7–8, 9, 51, 74–75; editorial quality of, 27–28; and literary genres, 15–16, 25–28; and oral narrative form, 1–2, 73–81; and political movements, 10–11, 25; and postcolonial theory, 9–10; and protest tradition, 7; representativeness of, 17–18; as resistance literature, 7, 10–11, 24, 75, 126; as self-representation, 9, 14, 27, 31–32, 49–50, 53; therapeutic/healing function of, 20, 25, 64, 66n9; and traditional stories, 76–79; by women, 69, 70–73. *See also* genres, literary; narrative forms; *see also individual works*

Aboriginal rights movement/political organizations, 8–9, 10–11, 16–17, 25, 29–30, 100n7

"Aboriginal Sin" (Peltier), 34–35, 85

Aboriginal spirituality/cosmology: as accepted by judicial system, 127; in "Ballad of Ron Cooper," 79–80; of Joe, 109–10; of Johnson, 59, 65; in *Kiss of the Fur Queen*, 106–107; Peltier on, 35–37, 125; in prison, 6, 25, 80. *See also* Christian doctrine/teachings

Aboriginal writers, as representatives of their people: Joe, 109; Johnson, 61, 63; Ms. Cree, 71, 73; Peltier, 6, 26, 32–34, 46; Willis, 86, 116, 121

Aboriginal writing: and colonization/dispossession, 2–3, 7–8, 9, 51; and

Books in the Aboriginal Studies Series
Published by Wilfrid Laurier University Press

Blockades and Resistance: Studies in Actions of Peace and the Temagami Blockades of 1988–89 / Bruce W. Hodgins, Ute Lischke, and David T. McNab, editors / 2003 / xi + 276 pp. / map, illustrations / ISBN 0-88920-381-4

Indian Country: Essays on Contemporary Native Culture / Gail Guthrie Valaskakis / 2005 / x + 293 pp. / photos / ISBN 0-88920-479-9

Walking a Tightrope: Aboriginal People and Their Representations / Ute Lischke and David T. McNab, editors / 2005 / xix + 377 pp. / photos / ISBN 978-0-88920-484-3

The Long Journey of a Forgotten People: Métis Identities and Family Histories / Ute Lischke and David T. McNab, editors / 2007 / viii + 386 pp. / maps, photos / ISBN 978-0-88920-523-9

Words of the Huron / John L. Steckley / 2007 / xvii + 259 pp. / ISBN 978-0-88920-516-1

Essential Song: Three Decades of Northern Cree Music / Lynn Whidden / 2007 / xvi + 176 pp. / photos, musical examples, audio CD / ISBN 978-0-88920-459-1

From the Iron House: Imprisonment in First Nations Writing / Deena Rymhs / 2008 / ix + 152 pp. / ISBN 978-1-55458-021-7